THRIVE

Don't Just Survive The Coming Collapse

NATHAN MACHAIN

1
I AM THE 1%

As of today, it is estimated that ONLY 1% of the population prepares for and stores up for what they will need in order to survive a true calamity. This means a huge majority of the population fails to have much of anything if and WHEN what they need each day to live evaporates. Most people have no clue what life will be like after the grocery stores close. They simply cannot grasp the horrors that will befall those people that have not put away for tomorrow or prepared contingencies for life threatening emergencies.

Instead of taking some time, effort, and money to safeguard themselves and their families, they have a wide array of excuses (or excuse me, reasons) for why preparing is crazy and unnecessary.

Oh come on, something like this could NEVER happen in MY area. The overall odds increase of having a mega, or even lesser, catastrophe as our population explodes in size. Just like increasing the size of a target, it is easier and more likely to get hit. Even if your area doesn't get hit, your location can be cut-off from getting vital supplies from areas that DID get hit. Every single spot on the planet is a potential target from such things as natural disasters, terrorism, war, pandemics, to a "black swan event"; and of course, this list can go on and on. No one is invulnerable, and living unrealistically is delusional and totally unsustainable.

Even if something happens, there is plenty of food and supplies for everyone in my city. Have you ever seen towns and cities cut off by winter storms? Supermarkets, food-warehouse stores, and restaurants are extremely limited—perhaps one to seven days of food are available at best. To prove this, take the population where you live and divide it by the number of grocery stores in your city or town. Now, go inside one of these stores and look around. Consider how fast a few hundred or a few thousand people could empty those shelves. I'm sure that you have seen the daily deliveries, carrying food and supplies for these stores. Imagine if these deliveries were to cease—what would happen then?

My state government, my community, and my neighbors will not abandon me and let me starve. It's a pure numbers game. If food and other necessities are not there for the state to distribute, then everyone who has failed to put away for such a disaster will go hungry. Your neighbors are likely to be in the same boat as you are, considering the fact that 99% of people don't prep. Those that did prepare are likely not to share with a bunch of people that chose not to. Taking food from those that did store up will not be an easy task, as they will likely be well-armed. It is extremely selfish to expect your neighbor to sacrifice their family's well-being just because you determined that preparing ahead of time would cramp your style. Simply put, don't be that 99%!

I have lots of credit cards; I will purchase anything I need in my city or nearby cities. First of all, credit is something that ONLY works when systems connected to the outside world function properly. People think that these little, "magical" pieces of plastic will save them in all circumstances. This misconception is something that will flatten those who go out and try to buy food, because by that time the banks will not allow, or will not be able to, process any credit or debit cards. Cash is necessary for buying what you need—have a fair amount in ALL denominations, from 20s down to 1s. Additionally, if your back-up plan is to drive to another city to purchase emergency supplies, you may not be able to get out of your area due to lack of fuel or closed roads. Again, have your own supplies BEFORE disaster strikes.

There is no room to store supplies that will never be used anyway. Vertical storage is one way that even very limited amounts of space can be used to put away what someone needs. There are all sorts of "dead spaces" around the house. Under the bed, closet shelves, or your garage are just a few ideas. Just look around; be creative. Square footage of a home is two dimensional, as there is usually about 8 ft. of space between ceiling to floor. Even people living in tiny apartments can find room to store up emergency needs.

It's just too much work to bother with. Even a person that is hardly an expert prepper, who has stored-up something, will fare far better than the 99% that have stored-up nothing. Simply picking-up some extra food and supplies at the market each time you go and putting these into boxes in some isolated part of the home will add a significant reserve. This limited effort will reap huge rewards WHEN you need them most.

I have absolutely no idea what to store or how much. What do you use on a day-to-day basis? This is what you want to store. Buy your regular household staples in jars, bottles, or well-sealed packages for longer-term storage. How much to store can be determined simply by asking yourself, "How long do I want to be self-sufficient during a disaster?" Have a time frame—a month, two months, etc. You should be able to easily identify how much of something you will use in a certain amount of time.

I don't need any protection after a disaster; the police, National Guard, and military will protect me. Even those that don't like firearms should consider owning one. The larger the distance between an attacker and your family, the less chance that someone you love will get injured or killed. A firearm gives you that distance. At least have something to defend yourself and your family with. There are some real psychos out there that will certainly take advantage of the lawlessness that will come with no police or military force. How many police does your city have per citizen? This ratio is one golden reason to have self-protection before, during, and after a disaster. Also, there may be no way of reaching law enforcement, even if they are available after a true disaster, as cell towers and phone lines may be fried.

I have a good car and family in other areas. If anything happens, I will just go and stay with them. One of the worst assumptions is that family or friends will openly accept you and yours. Even if they do, you may not be able to get to them. Your car or vehicle may be disabled for any number of reasons, or the roads may be impassable due to destruction or closure by law enforcement. Remaining securely at your present location should always be your first goal. Bug-out only as a last resort (unless you have a complete bug-out strategy and destination already in place ahead of time).

I work all week long and am going to spend my extra money on fun rather than fear. Self-indulgences seldom have much, if any, lasting benefit. People often blow their money on something that was nothing more than fleeting fun. In the end, it is often expensive and worthless. A sensible plan is to do anything that will bring long-term enjoyment, that will help you and your family live your lives with less short-term and long-term stress. The amount of anxiety you and your family will suffer after a true disaster strikes and you have nothing to feed yourself and your family with will be well beyond what any job or most of life's agonies can bring. Entertainment can give you temporal enjoyment, but not having the necessities you need in an emergency will end your life in true anguish.

Survival and prepping is living in a negative mindset, and as long as I stay positive, only positive things will happen to me. One of the most positive things that can come out of a crisis is to have what you need when the situation arises. Also, in a humanitarian sense, if you can't help yourself, then you certainly can't help others. Too many people live like the proverbial ostrich with its head buried in the sand. Hoping that the economy will never collapse, or that a mega earthquake won't hit an area that is way overdue, or that wars will come to a halt, and so on and so on, is not a realistic approach. Remember, your hope should only be in God! He alone gives the knowledge and wherewithal to prepare wisely. Let God guide you in this weighty endeavor. What could be better than peace of mind?

If we become sick after a disaster, we have good medical treatment centers that will care for us. Medical response could be overwhelmed and could takes days or weeks to come back online. It is likely that the number one killer after a calamity will be disease. Preventive care for you and your family is all too essential. Germ control and proper sanitation are top priorities here. Storage of anti-bacterial soaps, bleach, wet-wipes, hand-sanitizers, and other disinfectants are something no home should be without. Most disease will be water-borne, so it is critical to know how to filter and/or disinfect your water in order to ensure it is potable. Investment in a really well-stocked first-aid kit is an excellent survival item as well.

If a disaster hits, everybody will band together and save the day. This thought is a nice sentiment, but throughout history this romanticism has proven to be less of a reality. With a bad enough disaster, hope of recovery will be stripped away, and people will revert back to the survival of the fittest mentality. Depending on the good will of human nature can and does lead to vast disappointment and more importantly, individual disaster. Depending on God to direct you correctly in regard to storing adequate provisions will ensure stability and reliability when needed most.

FEMA, the Red Cross, and other government agencies are huge. They have it covered. Even if these organizations and government agencies can get to you, their supplies will be severely limited, much like local- and state-run emergency-preparedness centers. Try to envision millions of people needing food, clean water, and a host of other supplies. The logistics of distribution on this scale is a nightmare for any agency planner. Even if there were enough rations, picture yourself standing in a 4–10 hour long line to get some crumbs and a drink of water. Instead, imagine yourself easily going into a back room of your house and simply getting what you need. This kind of puts things into perspective now, doesn't it?

There is always time to prepare. **What's the big rush?** No, there isn't always time. Eventually time will run out. Eventually that day will come when national and/or world events will deteriorate to such a point that hoarding, rioting, and chaos will ensue. The best time to start preparing was yesterday, and the next best time is right now. Every day that goes by without putting away what you need means less and less resources for that ever fateful day that is fast approaching. Start preparing today, and find out just how satisfying it is when you have exactly what you need right at your fingertips.

The decision is yours. You have read the most common reasons cited by the 99% for not preparing. You have two choices and two alone; either cling to this make-believe notion that the bubble will never burst or look beyond the present with a thoughtful and pragmatic approach. You can either be the ant or the vulture. I think the choice is clear, don't you?

King Solomon put it best: Go to the ant, you sluggard; consider its ways and be wise! It has no commander, no overseer or ruler, yet it stores its provisions in summer and gathers its food at harvest. How long will you lie there, you sluggard? When will you get up from your sleep? (Proverbs 6:6-9)

2
THE PSYCHOLOGY OF SURVIVAL

Some people with survival training have not used their skills and have died as a consequence. A key ingredient in any survival situation is the mental attitude of the individual involved. Having survival skills is important, but having the will to survive is essential. Without a desire to survive, acquired skills serve little purpose and invaluable knowledge goes to waste.

There is a psychology to survival. You will face many stressors in a survival environment that will ultimately affect your mind. These stressors can produce thoughts and emotions that, if poorly understood, can transform a confident, well-trained person into an indecisive, ineffectual individual with questionable ability to survive. Thus, you must be aware of and be able to recognize those stressors commonly associated with survival. It is also imperative that you be aware of your reactions to the wide variety of stressors associated with survival.

A Look at Stress
Before we can understand what our psychological reactions would be in a survival setting, it is helpful to first know a little bit about stress and its effects. Stress is not a disease that you can cure and eliminate. Instead, it is a condition we all experience. Stress can be described as our reaction to pressure. It is the name given to the experience we have as we physically, mentally, emotionally, and spiritually respond to life's tensions.

Need for stress

We need stress because it has many positive benefits. Stress provides us with challenges; it gives us chances to learn about our values and strengths. Stress can show our ability to handle pressure without breaking. It tests our adaptability and flexibility and can stimulate us to do our best. Because we usually do not consider unimportant events stressful, stress can also be an excellent indicator of the significance we attach to an event—in other words, it highlights what is important to us.

We need to have some stress in our lives, but too much of anything can be bad. The goal is to have stress, but not an excess of it. Too much stress can take its toll on people and organizations. Too much stress leads to distress. Distress causes an uncomfortable tension that we try to escape or preferably avoid. Listed below are a few of the common signs of distress that you may encounter when faced with too much stress:

- Difficulty making decisions
- Angry outbursts
- Forgetfulness
- Low-energy level
- Constant worrying
- Propensity for mistakes
- Thoughts about death or suicide
- Trouble getting along with others
- Withdrawing from others
- Hiding from responsibilities
- Carelessness

Survival Stressors

Any event can lead to stress and as everyone has experienced, events don't always come one at a time. Often, stressful events occur simultaneously. These events are not stress, but they produce it and are called "stressors." Stressors are the obvious cause while stress is the response. Once the body recognizes the presence of a stressor, it then begins to act to protect itself.

In response to a stressor, the body prepares either to "fight or flee." This preparation involves an internal SOS sent throughout the body. As the body responds to this SOS, the following actions take place:

- The body releases stored fuels (sugar and fats) to provide quick energy.
- Breathing rate increases to supply more oxygen to the blood.
- Muscle tension increases to prepare for action.
- Blood-clotting mechanisms are activated to reduce bleeding from cuts.

- Senses become more acute (hearing becomes more sensitive, pupils dilate, smell becomes sharper) so that you are more aware of your surroundings.
- Heart rate and blood pressure rise to provide more blood to the muscles.

This protective posture lets you cope with potential dangers. However, you cannot maintain this level of alertness indefinitely.

Stressors are not courteous; one stressor does not leave because another one arrives. Stressors add-up. The cumulative effect of minor stressors can be a major distress if they all happen too close together. As the body's resistance to stress wears down and the sources of stress continue (or increase), eventually a state of exhaustion arrives. At this point, the ability to resist stress or use it in a positive way gives out and signs of distress appear. Anticipating stressors and developing strategies to cope with them are two ingredients in the effective management of stress. Therefore, it is essential that you be aware of the types of stressors that you will encounter. The following paragraphs explain a few of these.

Injury, Illness, or Death
Injury, illness, and death are real possibilities that you may have to face during a major catastrophe. Perhaps nothing is more stressful than being alone in an unfamiliar environment where you could die from hostile action, an accident, or from eating something lethal, such as in a bug-out scenario. Illness and injury can also add to stress by limiting your ability to maneuver, get food and drink, find shelter, and defend yourself. Even if illness and injury don't lead to death, they add to stress

through the pain and discomfort they generate. It is only by controlling the stress associated with the vulnerability to injury, illness, and death that you can have the courage to take the risks associated with survival tasks.

Uncertainty and Lack of Control
Some people have trouble operating in settings where everything is not clear-cut. The only guarantee in a survival situation is that nothing is guaranteed. It can be extremely stressful operating on limited information in a setting where you have limited control of your surroundings. This uncertainty and lack of control also add to the stress of potentially becoming ill, injured, or killed.

Environment
Even under the most ideal circumstances, nature is quite formidable. In wilderness survival, you will have to contend with the stressors of weather, terrain, and the variety of creatures inhabiting an area. Heat, cold, rain, winds, mountains, swamps, deserts, insects, dangerous reptiles, and other animals are just a few of the challenges that you will encounter while working to survive. Depending on how you handle the stress of your environment, your surroundings can be either a source of food and protection or can be a cause of extreme discomfort leading to injury, illness, or death. Although this brings to mind outdoor survival, imagine if you must flee due to massive civil unrest or lack of continued resources; then, the elements will come into play. However, even with hunkering-down, climate certainly is a factor, for what is you live in the desert and calamity befalls you in the summer when it is 100 degrees or more, and there is no electricity to run air-conditioning or fans?

How about living in the mountains or in the North during winter, what if the gas goes out, and the temperature is in the negative digits. How would you survive then?

Hunger and Thirst
Without food and water you will weaken and eventually die. Thus, getting and preserving food and water takes on increasing importance as the length of time in a survival setting increases. Scavenging and/or rationing can also be a big source of stress since we are used to having an abundant supply of water and food at present.

Fatigue
Forcing yourself to continue surviving is not easy as you grow more tired and weak. It is possible to become so fatigued that the act of just staying awake is stressful in itself.

Isolation
There are some advantages to facing adversity with others. We may have self-taught, individual skills, but most people are more comfortable with a team approach. Although we complain about pet peeves, we become used to the information and guidance given by others, especially during times of confusion. Being in contact with others also provides a greater sense of security and a feeling someone is available to help if problems occur. A significant stressor in survival situations is that of having to rely solely on your own resources when somehow separated from the group.

Fear and Anxiety
If you are trying to survive, fear can have a positive function if it encourages you to be cautious in situations where recklessness could result in

injury. Unfortunately, fear can also immobilize you. It can cause you to become so frightened that you fail to perform activities essential for survival. Most people will have some degree of fear when placed in unfamiliar surroundings under adverse conditions. There is no shame in this! You must train yourself not to be overcome by your fears. Associated with fear is anxiety. Because it is natural for you to be afraid, it is also natural for you to experience anxiety. When used in a healthy way, anxiety can urge you to act to end, or at least master, the dangers that threaten your existence. If you were never anxious, there would be little motivation to make changes in your life. In a survival setting you can reduce your anxiety by performing those tasks that will ensure you come through the ordeal alive. As you reduce your anxiety, you also bring under control the source of that anxiety—your fears. In this form, anxiety is good; however, anxiety can also have a devastating impact. Anxiety can overwhelm you to the point where you become easily confused and have difficulty thinking. Once this happens, it will become increasingly difficult for you to make good judgments and sound decisions. To survive, you must learn techniques to calm your anxieties and keep them in the range where they help, not hurt.

Frustration and Anger
Frustration arises when you are continually thwarted in your attempts to reach a goal. The goal of survival is to stay alive until you can reach help or until help can reach you. To achieve this goal, you must complete some tasks with minimal resources. It is inevitable, in trying to do these tasks, that something will go wrong; that something will happen beyond your control; and that with your life at stake, every mistake is

magnified in terms of its importance. Thus, eventually, you will have to cope with frustration when a few of your plans run into trouble. One outgrowth of this frustration is anger. Frustration and anger generate impulsive reactions, irrational behavior, poorly thought-out decisions, and, in some instances, an "I quit" attitude (people sometimes avoid doing something they can't master). If you can harness and properly channel the emotional intensity associated with anger and frustration, you can productively act as you answer the challenges of survival. If you do not properly focus your angry feelings, you can waste much energy in activities that do little to further either your chances of survival or the chances of those around you.

Depression and Guilt
You would be a rare person indeed if you did not get sad, at least momentarily, when faced with the hardships of survival. As this sadness deepens, it becomes "depression." Depression is closely linked with frustration and anger. Frustration will cause you to become increasingly angry as you fail to reach your goals. If the anger does not help you succeed, then the frustration level goes even higher. A destructive cycle between anger and frustration will continue until you become worn down—physically, emotionally, and mentally. When you reach this point, you start to give up, and your focus shifts from "What can I do?" to "There is nothing I can do." Depression is an expression of this hopeless, helpless feeling. Thoughts that give you the desire to try harder and live one more day are the ones to focus on. Do not allow yourself to sink into a depressed state, which can sap you of all of your energy and, more importantly, your will to survive. It is imperative that you resist yielding

to depression.

The circumstances leading to a survival situation are often dramatic and tragic. While naturally relieved to be alive, you simultaneously may be mourning the deaths of others who were less fortunate. It is not uncommon for survivors to feel guilty about being spared from death while others were not. Allow this feeling to turn into the great honor of living for some greater purpose in life and to carry-on the work of those killed. Whatever reasons you give yourself, do not let feelings of guilt prevent you from living. God created you with a purpose in mind and will have spared your life for a greater calling. The living who abandon their chance to survive accomplish nothing. Such an act would be the greatest tragedy.

Loneliness and Boredom
Man is a social animal. Human beings enjoy the company of others. Very few people want to be alone all the time! There is a distinct chance of isolation in a survival setting. Isolation is not bad. Loneliness and boredom can bring to the surface qualities you thought only others had. The extent of your imagination and creativity may surprise you. When required to do so, you may discover some hidden talents and abilities. Most of all, you may tap into a reservoir of inner strength and fortitude you never knew you had. "If God is for us, who can be against us?" (Romans 8:31). Conversely, loneliness and boredom can be another source of depression. If you are surviving alone, or with others, you must find ways to keep your mind productively occupied.

Preparing yourself
Your mission in a survival situation is to stay alive.

Remember, survival is natural to everyone; being unexpectedly thrust into the life-or-death struggle of survival is not. Do not be afraid of your "natural reactions to this unnatural situation." Prepare yourself to rule over these reactions so they serve your ultimate interest of staying alive with honor and dignity.

Know Yourself
You should take the time through training, family, and friends to discover who you are on the inside. Strengthen your stronger qualities and develop the areas that you know are currently a weakness.

Anticipate fears
Don't pretend that you will have no fears. Begin thinking about what would frighten you the most in a survival situation. Train in those areas of concern. The goal is not to eliminate the fear, but to build confidence in your ability to function despite your fears. "Do not fear, for I am with you; Do not anxiously look about you, for I am your God. I will strengthen you, surely I will help you, Surely I will uphold you with My righteous right hand" (Isaiah 41:10).

Be realistic
Don't be afraid to make an honest appraisal of situations. See circumstances as they are, not as you want them to be. When you go into a survival setting with unrealistic expectations, you may be laying the groundwork for bitter disappointment. Follow the adage, "Hope for the best, prepare for the worst."

Adopt a positive attitude
Learn to see the potential good in everything. Looking for the good not only boosts morale, it also

is excellent exercise for your strength of mind.

Remind yourself what is at stake
Failure to prepare yourself psychologically can lead to depression, carelessness, inattention to detail, loss of confidence, poor decision making, and giving-up before the body gives-up. Remember that your life and the lives of others who depend on you are at stake.

Train
Through training and life experiences, begin today to prepare yourself to cope with the rigors of survival. Demonstrating your skills in training will give you the confidence to call upon them should the need arise. Remember, the more realistic the training, the less overwhelming an actual survival setting will be.

Learn stress management techniques
Learning stress management techniques can significantly enhance your capability to remain calm and focused as you work to keep yourself and others alive. A few good techniques to develop include relaxation, time management, assertiveness, and cognitive restructuring skills (the ability to control how you view a situation). Remember, the will to survive can also be considered the refusal to give up.

3
SURVIVAL KITS

The best bug-out bag is the one that is accessible, lightweight, and tailored to suit your individual needs. Many people automatically assume that in a crisis, their car will bring them a sure escape. In a true bug-out situation, roads will be gridlocked and jammed.

If you recall back to video shots during Hurricane Katrina and the lines of cars attempting to escape the impending hurricane, you will certainly understand what I mean.

I admit it, I am a backpack junkie. I have more backpacks than many women have purses. The good news is that since I'm a preparedness writer and teacher, I can rationalize that concept all day long. Finding the perfect backpack is a journey, not a destination. You're going to try and buy many before you find that perfect pack, and even then it may not be perfect for all circumstances.

BOB (Bug Out Bag)

A bug-out bag is a portable survival kit that contains all the basic, life-sustaining items, theoretically, that you would need in order to survive for three days. The focus is on evacuation, rather than on long-term survival. It's a good idea to have one for each family member and ensure that it's always ready to go.

What to place in your BOB is highly subjective and dependent upon what kind of survival situation you will find yourself in. Your carried water supply should be top priority; a lot of your survival is based upon how much water you can carry for those 72 hours.

This kit is also referred to as a 72-hour bag, a get-out-of-dodge bag (GOOD Bag), an EVAC bag, and a battle box.

EDC (every-day carry)

Essentially, your EDC equipment is just a group of tools. The tools you need depend on the circumstances that you will find yourself in and what problems you're trying to solve. The key to this is predicting situations that you may find yourself in first and then finding the tools that will solve those predicaments. Your EDC gear will change as you and your lifestyle change—maybe you find new things that you want to carry or maybe your new job goes from office to outdoors or vice versa. Maybe you pick-up a new hobby, like boating or snow skiing. You are going to carry different things depending on if you are walking into a board meeting versus going to the beach with your family. What kind of outfit are you going to be wearing? What problems might you encounter wherever you will be going? It's basically the stuff you have with you every day. If you are a student, it may be your school backpack, if you are an executive, it may be your briefcase, if you are a young, hip male, it may be your messenger bag, or if you are a woman, your EDC will DEFINITELY be your purse. In a lot of cases, it's not even a pack or a case, but the items you keep in your pockets, on your keychain, in your wallet, on your belt, or around your neck.

GHB (Get-Home Bag)

A get-home bag is what you carry with you or put in your car if you're out somewhere, and for whatever reason, you have to hump it back home with the needed supplies for the trek.

Vehicle Survival Bag or Container

Your car bag/container should always have essentials for car repair and first-aid, but you should keep a survival kit in it as well, in case you're caught out-and-about without your main bug-out bag or if you break down with another person in the car who has to survive with you. My

Jeep has enough survival and medical equipment in it for me to survive even if I break down in the middle of the desert for a couple of days. This set up will be covered in more detail in the next chapter.

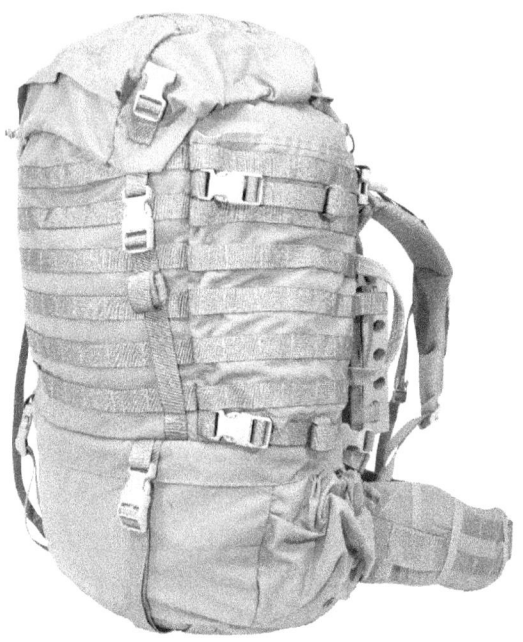

INCH (I'm never coming home) Bag

This is the biggest of the bunch. My INCH bag is definitely separate from my other bags and is kept in an easy-to-get-to location. It's essentially a bug-out bag on steroids and is designed to be put into whatever vehicle I'm traveling in when I have to get-out-of-Dodge.

The INCH bag is the pack of last resort. Unlike the BOB or EDC bag, the "I'm never coming home" pack is for situations that dictate that one leave the homestead and effectively become a refugee.

An INCH bag should differ from a BOB in that it must sustain you indefinitely. The purpose of the INCH bag is to give you time to survive elsewhere or get you to an alternate survival location so that at some point in the future, when the recovery process has been completed, you can return home. However, prepare your INCH bag as though you will never be coming back home, because there are certainly no guarantees. For instance, you would probably pack several days of rations in your BOB, as this type of pack should have enough room for 72-hrs worth of food. However, with the INCH bag, you would probably only carry minimal rations, but focus more importantly on ways to procure food by carrying such things as a fishing kit, traps, snares, seeds, etc., since you can't carry enough food and rations for an indefinite period of time.

Another example to consider would be in reference to shelters. A BOB would probably just include a poncho and wool blanket, as you would only need cover for three days. An INCH bag, on the other hand, would require a light-weight tent and light-weight sleeping bag, and a roll-up sleeping pad for long-term ground insulation, to be used under your sleeping bag. You would also include tools in this type of bag, such as a folding saw and small axe for processing wood, for creating more permanent shelters.

What size?
What size backpack will be right for you? Are you a large person, a petite person, or a 7-foot-tall giant?

How do we solve this dilemma? Let's first figure out what factors or metrics are the most important in order to answer that question—then and only then can we begin this quest.

Volume: Cubic Inches?

There is much confusion out there when trying to determine the true capacity of backpacks. Many packs will claim the exact same capacity as another, but when testing them out, I find that one backpack holds much more gear than the other. It is somewhat baffling; more so, because the process for measuring backpack capacity has been standardized for so many years.

The standard for determining the capacity of a backpack entails using 20mm, plastic balls as the filler. Packs are loaded up and then emptied. The 20mm balls are henceforth dumped into a measuring device. According to this standard, capacity measurements should not include any compartments that are not entirely sealed by zippers, such as shovel pockets, bottle holders, compression pockets, etc. I suspect that some of the overstated backpack capacities probably include the additional capacity of these pockets. This makes online backpack shopping extremely frustrating, since there is no ability, of course, to compare the sizes in person.

General Sizing (in no way an exact science)

- Every-day carry (EDC) will be under 1,000-cubic inches
- Get-home bag (GHB) packs are typically 1,500- to 2,000-cubic inches
- Bug-out bags (BOB) range from 2,000- to 3,500-cubic inches

- I'm-never-coming-home (INCH) bag is 4,000-cubic inches and up

Packs by Size

- **Maxpedition Fatboy Versipack** is 236 cu. in.
- **Maxpedition Falcon-II** is 1,520 cu. in.
- **ALICE pack** (medium size) external- frame pack is 2,350 cu. in. (military surplus)
- **5.11 Tactical Rush 72 backpack** is 2,894 cu. in.
- **Teton Sports Scout 3400** internal-frame pack is 3,400 cu. in.
- **ALICE pack** (large size) external-frame pack is 3,800 cu. in. (military surplus)
- **Kelty Trekker** external-frame pack is 3,950 cu. in.
- **High Sierra 75 liter** internal-frame pack (Classic series 59501 Appalachian) is 4,580 cu. in.
- **US Army Molle II Large RuckSack** external-frame pack is 5,000 cu. in. (military surplus)
- **ALPS OutdoorZ Commander Freighter frame-plus-pack bag** is 5,250 cu. in.
- **ILBE (improved load-bearing equipment)** internal-frame pack is a camouflage, USMC–MARPAT pattern, 4,500 cu. in. main rucksack. It can be mated with an additional 1,500 cu. in. assault pack, along with a 100 oz. hydration bladder. This will give you 6,000+ cu. in. of space for the full system (military surplus).
- **FILBE (family of improved load-bearing equipment)** external-frame pack is a coyote tan, USMC, 5,000 cu. in. main rucksack. This latest generation replace-

ment of the ILBE is in current use by our USMC. You can purchase this setup off eBay or Amazon. It can be mated with an additional 2,300 cu. in. assault pack, along with a 100 oz. hydration carrier. This will give you 7,300+ cu. in. for the full system (military surplus).

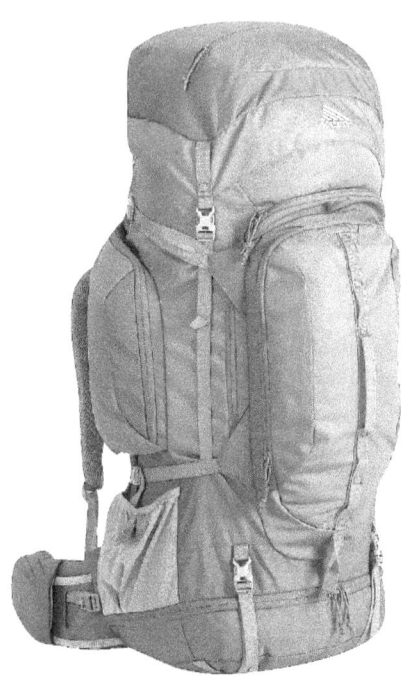

Internal-Frame Backpacks

Internal-frame backpacks are fairly popular because they use a hidden metal- (usually aluminum) or composite frame that supports the backpack from the inside. The frame is used to help place the weight on your hips, where your body can most effectively carry it.

An internal-frame backpack typically has a narrower profile and is generally positioned behind the shoulder harness. The frame does provide some stiffness, but it still offers an amount of flexibility, which will allow the pack to move as your body moves. Internal-frame backpacks are slimmer, providing you more room to maneuver your arms for climbing and other activities.

An internal-frame backpack should hold the load closer to your center of gravity, which is key to maintaining your balance.

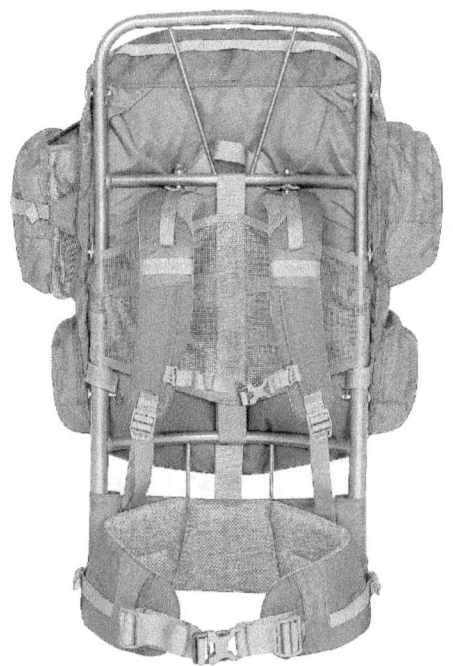

External-Frame Backpacks

An external-frame backpack is pretty much a backpack on an aluminum-tube frame.

External-frame backpacks are rigid and strong. They are generally heavier than internal-frame backpacks; however, with increases in technology and plastics, lighter-weight models have become readily available.

A feature that I enjoy on the external-frame backpacks is that the load can be expanded more easily by strapping items, such as tents, sleeping bags, and other items, directly onto the frame.

There's typically more space between the frame and your back too, preventing your back from becoming extra sweaty.

Materials and Construction

This is why seeing a bag in person makes shopping so much easier. You can typically tell by a quick, visual inspection and by a simple touch if the material is cheap and may easily rip. This is why a great seller, such as Amazon, makes all the difference in the world. If the bag arrives and is cheaply made or the zippers are a total fraud, you merely put it back in the box and ship it off to Amazon. Plus, the ability to read the reviews from other purchasers makes Amazon the reigning king in my book!

As a guide, I would recommend water- and abrasion-resistant, light-weight, ballistic-nylon, above-500-denier material, and seek out self-repairing, YKK zippers, and double-stitched stress points.

Color

If you wish to be stealthy during your bug out, choose a neutral-colored pack. You actually don't want to go all camouflage, because if you are seen, people will target you because you appear more tactical, thus, likely to be more prepared then they.

Neutral colors, such as earth-toned greens, greys, and browns, or just plain old black work well. You don't want to shout, "I'm a prepper," or scream, "I'm special forces." You just want to be.

How to Get Started
As I said earlier, choosing a bug-out backpack is a journey and not a destination. As long as you keep that mentality, you won't freak out and kick yourself every time you find a better bag than the one before it. You're going to buy and try many before you find that perfect pack, and even then it may not be perfect for all circumstances.

With that being said, the first thing that you need to do is get a bag. You may be wondering why? Why, you might ask, would I put the cart before the horse? I've seen lots of people pick what they need first and then get a bag to fit it all into. This, unfortunately, means picking a bag that suits your contents and not your back. You should get an idea of what kind of bag you're looking for and then fill it with whatever essential items will fit, being careful to leave some room for things you find along the way or other things you decide to pack later on.

By choosing the right bag, or set bags, you ensure that you will be able to carry your things for longer distances, with greater comfort at that. It will not do you any good to pack 80 lbs. of emergency gear, and then bug out, only to have to drop 50 lbs. of it because you can't carry it all. You need to practice wearing your gear in whatever terrain you might need it in. What you can put in it will be based on how much you can carry. (Don't forget how much water weighs, as you will definitely be carrying a lot of that along the way as well.)

Fitting a Pack

It is essential to have a pack that fits you suitably. The major measurements to consider are your spine length, hip size, and shoulder width. Using these measurements during pack selection will give you a pack with the correct length, one with an accurate-sized hip belt, and properly-fitted shoulder straps. Packs vary from company to company, so check the manufacturer's instructions for both fitting and loading. Packs are generally categorized into men's, women's, kids, and unisex groupings. The idea behind a frame pack is to have the frame transfer most of the weight to your legs through the hip belt. Therefore, when fitting a pack, the place to start with is the hip belt. A hip belt can drastically reduce shoulder and neck fatigue by supporting up to 90% of a pack's weight and centering that weight nearer the center of mass. I will not even consider a pack for personal use unless it has a hip belt.

Finding Your Torso and Hip Size

One of the keys to a comfortable backpack is to get a pack that is the right size (small, medium, or large) for you. Your torso length—not your height—is the key measurement; hip size can also be helpful.

Find Your Torso Length

To do so, you'll need a friend and a flexible tape measure.

- Have your friend locate the bony bump at the base of your neck, where the slope of your shoulder meets your neck. This is your 7th cervical (or C7) vertebra. Tilt your head forward to locate it more easily. This is the top of your torso length.
- Place your hands on top of your hip bones (also known as your iliac crest), with fingers pointing forward, thumbs in back. This is the "shelf" on which your pack will rest. The middle of an imaginary line drawn between your thumbs is the bottom of your torso length.

- Using the tape measure, your friend should measure the distance between the C7 and the imaginary line between your thumbs. Be sure you stand up straight when being measured. You now should have your torso length.

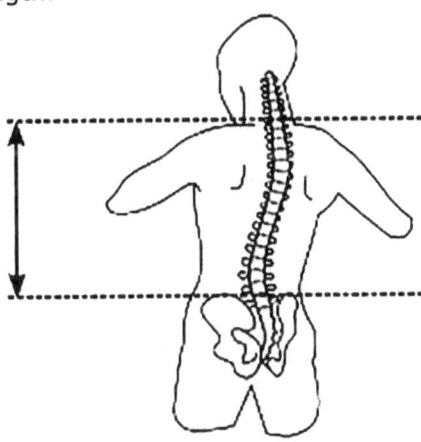

Use your torso length measurement to find your best pack size. Generally, manufacturers size their pack frames something like this:

- Extra Small: Fits torsos up to 15 ½ in.
- Small: Fits torsos 16 in. to 17½ in.
- Medium/Regular: Fits torsos 18 in. to 19½ in.
- Large/Tall: Fits torsos 20 in. and up

Determine Your Hip Size

While less important than torso length, your hip measurement is useful to know. It's especially helpful if you are considering a pack that offers interchangeable hip belts.

Take your tape measure and wrap it around the top of your hips. The correct measurement is along the "latitude line" that radiates out from your belly button to your sides and the high points of your hip bones. This is slightly higher than your waist, so your hip belt measurement may differ from your pants' waist size.

A properly positioned hip belt will straddle your hips about an inch above and below that latitude line, wrapping around the two, pointy, pelvic bones on the front of your body.

Preparing the Backpack

Place about 15 or 20 lb. of weight in the backpack. Anything will do—climbing ropes, liters of water, or whatever is on hand —just make sure the load is evenly distributed in the pack, with some of the weight up high. Also, make sure that the shoulder straps, waist belt (also referred to as a hip belt), and load straps are reasonably loose.

Tighten Shoulder Straps

After putting the backpack on, you'll first want to tighten the shoulder straps. This pulls the pack a little higher up on the hips.

Tighten Waist Belt

Cinch the waist belt up snuggly—not so much that you cut off circulation to your legs—but it will have to be somewhat tight to support the pack's weight. Your hips should carry the majority of the load.

Waist-Belt Positioning

Slip your fingers inside your waist belt and find your iliac crest. The top edge of the waist belt should be about 1 in. above the iliac crest.

Shoulder-Strap Positioning

Now, look at how the shoulder straps fit. If you're alone, get in front of a mirror and stand sideways. The shoulder straps should be flush with your shoulders and upper back. There should be very little space between the backside of your shoulders and the straps.

Poorly-Fitting Suspension

If there's too much space between the straps and your shoulders, this indicates the backpack's suspension isn't matching your torso length, and the distance between the shoulder straps and waist belt needs to be shortened. If the pack's suspension can't be shortened far enough, or if the backpack isn't adjustable, you'll need to try a shorter model.

If the shoulder straps are wrapping around your shoulders correctly, but the waist belt is positioned too high in relation to the iliac crest, then the distance between shoulder straps and waist belt needs to be increased.

Load Strap Positioning

The load straps attach the top section of the pack, to the uppermost portion of the shoulder straps.

Ideally, these straps should be at about 45-degree angles, although a 15-degree deviation is fine. Pull them to bring the pack a little closer to your body and to keep the load balanced over your hips, but don't yank on the load straps so hard that they cause the front of your shoulder straps to dig in. Play with the adjustments a bit until you find that sweet spot.

Sternum-Strap Fitting
Buckle the sternum strap and comfortably adjust the position to about 2 in. below your collar bones, and lightly cinch it down. This pulls the shoulder straps comfortably away from your armpit and centers them over your shoulders. Do not pull so tight that is hinders your breathing.

Proper Hiking Posture
Before we check to see where you're feeling the pack's weight, lean forward just a little, bending at the hips. This is how you'll normally carry a backpack. It's your body's way of maintaining balance by positioning the load over your own center of gravity (your hips). If you were to rigidly stand straight up, you'd discover that the bottom of the pack presses too much into the lumbar region of your lower back.

Where the Weight Should Fall
If the pack is fitted just right, the majority of the weight should be felt in the hip region, as opposed to your shoulders. No matter how strong your shoulders are, you don't want all the weight to fall there for hours on end. Your legs are much stronger and can easily support the extra weight of a fully-loaded backpack.

How to Pack a Backpack

Sizing & Fitting a Backpack
Learning how to organize your gear properly before loading your backpack will eliminate forgotten items and help you remove unnecessary luxuries. In addition, efficiently packing your backpack will give you more comfort, convenience, and stability.

Backpack-Weight Distribution
By distributing weight in a specific manner, you can achieve better comfort, convenience, and stability. Instead of simply stuffing your backpacking gear inside your bag, follow these guidelines.

Internal backpacks
Items with the most weight should be centered high between the shoulder blades and close to your back while trail hiking with an internal-frame pack. By doing this, the weight is placed on the hips, where it should be. When off the trail, items should be placed a bit lower on the back, lowering your center of gravity and stabilizing you better on rough terrain.

External backpacks
External backpacks are recommended for trail hiking. The heaviest items should be packed on top and closest to the back to center the pack's weight over the hips and help you stay in a more upright stance.

Packing Tips
Either frame type you choose, medium-weight gear should be placed in the middle and furthest from the back. Lightweight items should be placed lowest in the backpack.

Be careful not to overload your pack, or your body at that. A loaded backpack shouldn't exceed 25% to 30% of your ideal body weight. Although this is a general guideline, some experienced backpackers may be able to carry more weight. Beginner backpackers, and less-fit persons, should start with less weight.

Backpack Organization
In order to pack your backpack in an organized fashion, you may want to lay out all of your backpacking equipment. This is a great way to make sure that you have all of your gear. It also ensures that all of your supplies are sorted by weigh—light, medium, and heavy. Another good idea is to cluster small, similar items, such as eating utensils and pots, all together in Ziploc or stuff bags. Remember to store food and anything liquid in sealed bags to prevent messes and spills.

When packing your backpack, be sure to fill in all empty space with small or compressible items. For example, you can stuff a shirt inside a pot, or remove your sleeping bag from its sack and stuff it around other gear.

After your bag is loaded and packed, tighten all compression straps to limit load-shifting while hiking. On top of that, I like to give my pack a few hard shakes to help the load settle in, then tighten the straps further—but not to the point of deforming the pack shape or damaging the contents.

Make it a point to check the contents of your kit at least once every season. Weed-out old items that may have leaked, dried-up, expired, or aren't worth their weight anymore. Practice with your contents until you are confident in using them. Don't wait until an emergency or disaster to start packing. If you do not want to have a packed bag, make a list of everything you need and keep the list in the pack. At the very least, have all of your items inventoried so that you know where everything is, (but I strongly suggest you keep it packed and easily assessable for grab-and-go). Always test run your pack by loading your actual equipment and going on a hike on various terrains.

Don't forget about your kiddos; even though you will end up carrying most of your kids' supplies, they can still use a small bag where they can store their snacks, water, small toys, or a stuffed animal. This will give them a sense of comfort and security during a time when they need it most.

GENERAL PACKING SUGGESTIONS

- A general rule of thumb is that 50% of the weight should be in the upper third of the pack.
- For consistently steep or rough terrain, carry the weight lower to give you better balance.
- The horizontal weight distribution should be balanced so that the left side of the pack is in balance with the right.
- Your hip belt should have enough room to allow you to loosen or tighten it for different layers of clothing beneath. If the belt is too loose, socks or shirts can be inserted between the belt and your body. This adds

an extra layer of padding to the belt as well, which may increase the comfort of the fit.

- Avoid hanging things all over the outside of your pack—not only does no one want to listen to you clink, clank, and clunk your way down the trail, all that noise will certainly make you a very easy target! In addition to that, all that junk can snag branches. If you find yourself having to tie things off and on all the time, either your pack is too small or you are carrying too much (or both).

- Think about the things you will need during the day and have them relatively accessible so that it doesn't take a complete emptying of your pack to find lunch, the first-aid kit, or your rain gear. Also, group and store items according to function. For example, keep toiletries together in small stuff sacks and store your GPS/maps, knife, etc. inside a front pocket, top lid, or in the top of the main compartment. This keeps essentials handy and easy to find.

- For protection from rain, line your sleeping-bag stuff sack and main-pack compartments with plastic garbage bags. These can be reused on subsequent trips and recycled when you are through with them. They also work as emergency shelters. Pack rain covers are also useful.

The Desired Result
Ideally, a well-loaded pack will:

- Feel balanced when resting on your hips.
- Feel cohesive, like a whole unit, with nothing shifting or swaying inside.

- Feel stable and predictable as you walk, at one with your upper body.

Pack Dangers

For the average person, a fully-loaded backpack should not weigh more than 25% of their overall body weight. For instance, a 200 lb. person (in good health) should, therefore, be carrying no more than 50 lbs.

Are you used to walking around for 20 mi. with 50 lbs. of weight on your back? Maybe you didn't realize how quickly everything in your pack would add-up to be more than you could possibly carry? Do you know how much 3 gal. of water weighs? This is the recommended amount needed for each person in order to last for 3 days—approx. 25 lbs. /person.

Having a BOB that is too heavy can cause injury very easily. Not only that, it can wear-you-out much faster and make running, something you may have to do when the zombies are hungry, very difficult to do. Also, unless your bag is packed correctly, your center of balance will be off, and you can just about forget doing any type of tactical movement.

Am I talking about a trained Navy SEAL or your average Mr. and Mrs. Joe Public? Let's be honest with ourselves; most of us have sedentary jobs and don't train daily with 50 lb. packs like the 10th Mountain Division. What about your children? Will they be able to carry all of the supplies needed on their backs as well?

The second cause for danger comes from conspicuousness. Remember that a total collapse scenario means that massive amounts of society are displaced, scared, hurting, and desperate. With a large pack on your back, you are a greater target. Folks may see you with that big pack full of supplies and goodies and be inclined to relieve you of that extra weight. If their children are freezing or starving and you are walking around with the Wal-Mart camping section attached to your back, in bright orange, nonetheless, they may decide that you need that less than they do.

How can we avoid this problem?
Do you recall what we discussed earlier—pack smarter. A BOB should be viewed as a life preserver, not a convenience store. If all hell breaks loose in your town, what will you really need in order to survive? Will a change of clothes, something to shelter you from the elements, and a means to make a fire be what you mostly need or miscellaneous odds and ends? Add some food and water, with a back-up water filter for purifying water found elsewhere, and a simple first-aid kit, and you have most of the basics covered. Will all of this weigh significantly less than 50 pounds? It should. Personally, I pack all of those items, but the majority of them are in my INCH bag, not my BOB. Why? Simple—it's too much to carry. My INCH bag will be placed in my Jeep if the time ever comes to say goodbye to my sheltering-in-place plan. I pray it never comes down to that, but an INCH bag, in my opinion, is not something to bug-out with on your back; it is my Jeep's BOB, so weight and size is not as much of a factor.

What should be in your kit?

A preparedness bag is critical, but what is even more critical is what you put into it. When considering disaster preparedness, keep in mind that whatever survival gear and emergency supplies that are added to your bag can mean the difference between life and death, or at a minimum, determine your level of comfort.

Remember, however, that you can't carry as much as you think you can. The information that I'm about to give to you isn't a list of all the things you need to have—it's a list of all the things that you should CONSIDER. You should carry the least amount of things that you possibly can.

The type of environment you will be surviving in will determine the kind of items you will need. In preparing your survival gear, select items that are multipurpose, compact, lightweight, durable, and most importantly, functional. An item isn't worthy if it looks great but doesn't do what it is designed for.

If you're forced out of your home and need to survive on your own, remember the "core-4, basic-human-survival needs": shelter, water, fire, and food. Make sure your bag covers all of these.

Survival Supply Categories

- SAS survival pouch
- Food
- Medical
- Shelter
- Communications
- Fire
- Cooking
- Hygiene

- Tools
- Clothes
- Personal
- Money/Barter
- Weapons
- Baby/Child supplies
- Urban EDC Altoids tin

SAS Survival Pouch

The *SAS Survival Handbook* is a survival guide by British author and professional soldier, John Wiseman, and was first published in 1986. The book details how to survive in dangerous surroundings. One of the main items of preparedness discussed in this book is to always carry an SAS survival pouch, which contains useful gear/tools for a survival situation. Wiseman's survival skills are highly regarded almost universally amongst other survivalists. Due to this, I wanted to make sure to implement my own version of the SAS survival pouch in my personal, urban BOB.

Rather than using a military-style, rectangular pouch, as described by Wiseman in *the SAS Survival Handbook*, I decided to use a very common carrying case that I would normally never wear in an urban setting: the dreaded fanny pack! This fanny pack will be connected to my main, urban BOB using a carabiner.

It will be immediately disconnected and worn in an emergency situation. The purpose of this pouch is to ensure that you always have survival items on your person, even if you are out of contact with your primary bug-out bag. Since the fanny pack is a fairly common storage bag, although nerdy, it should not draw any unwanted attention while being worn.

- Fanny pack (high quality)
- Compact, LED flashlight
- Signal mirror
- Whistle
- Aluminum foil (heavy duty)
- Folding knife
- Ceramic escape knife/blade
- BIC lighter (mini)
- Mini can opener (P-38 military)
- Emergency mylar thermal blanket
- Four-function whistle (thermometer,magnifier,compass,and whistle)
- Waterproof matches
- Chewing gum (any brand)
- Flexible saw
- Flint steel
- Water-filter straw
- Water-treatment tablets
- Gorilla duct tape
- Mini Medi
- Pencil
- Roll-up water bottle (1L)
- Rite in the Rain notebook and pen
- Shemagh/bandanna
- Protein/Energy bars
- USB flash drive (8GB)
- WetFire tinder cubes
- Lock-picking set
- Universal handcuff key

Food

Include food items that have a decent shelf life and require little to no cooking.

- Protein/Energy bars
- MRE's/Dehydrated meals
- Emergency, 3600-calorie food bar
- Tuna pouches
- Jerky
- Rice pouches
- OvaEasy powdered eggs
- Instant oatmeal
- Ramen noodles/freeze-dried soups
- Trail mix
- Instant coffee/5-hour energy drink
- Hard candy
- Snickers

Medical

The Medical compartment is divided into four main sections: first aid, trauma, pharmacy, and tools. The equipment in this compartment should help cover any basic to intermediate medical needs in case of an emergency. In trauma situations, the items should hopefully grant me enough time to allow for professional medical assistance to take over.

- Scissors (mini)
- Fresnel lens
- Razor blade
- Safety Pins
- Scalpel
- Syringe
- Uncle Bills tweezers
- Acetaminophen

- Ibuprofen
- Naproxen
- Aspirin
- Benadryl
- Imodium AD
- Colloidal silver
- Oregano oil
- Tea tree oil
- Eye drops
- Vicodin (must be prescribed)
- Band-Aids (various sizes)
- BD Alcohol Swabs
- Benadryl Itch Relief Spray
- Nitrile exam gloves (non-latex)
- Burn-gel packets
- Gorilla super glue
- Medical tape (paper)
- Moleskin pads
- Neosporin
- Non-adherent dressing pads (different sizes)
- Petrolatum gauze dressing
- Rolled gauze
- Straws
- Surgical gauze sponges/gauze packing strip
- Steri-Strips
- Applicator sticks
- Dental repair kit
- Dental floss
- Mini mirror
- Q-tips
- Toothache medication
- Toothpicks
- Zilactin mouth-sore gel
- ABD pad
- ACE bandage
- Ammonia inhalants (x3)
- Laerdal CPR face shield

- Israeli Bandage
- Non-sterile triangular bandage
- QuickClot (50 gm)
- SOF Tactical Tourniquet
- Surgical masks
- N95/N100 respirator mask/ 3M P100 reusable respirator gas mask

Shelter

It is extremely important to have protection from the elements and have a warm, dry place to sleep. In a rural situation, I would have dedicated more weight to this particular compartment and included a tent and full size sleeping bag. However, in an urban setting, where there is often more concrete than woods, I decided to go with a minimalist approach. In the majority of my bug-out destinations, I will most likely have access to a house, shed, abandoned building, overpass, or other permanent structure. Due to this reason, I decided to concern myself more with an item such as an ultralight cot instead of something like a full-size tent. I will be including a tent in "Mrs. Prepper's" bug-out bag and will have a full-size sleeping bag possibly added to the urban BOB if deemed necessary.

- Tarp
- Ultra-light tarp pole set
- SOL thermal bivvy
- Ground cloth camping sheet (5x8 ft.)
- Grommet Tabs
- Ultra-light tent stakes
- Stake bag
- Therm-A-Rest Luxurylite ultralite cot

Communications

The communications' compartment contains all items used for not only communicating with others in my bug-out party, but also for gathering intel and alerting rescue-response teams. While there are many bug-out scenarios that will require you to be stealthy, the majority of bug-out scenarios in my preparedness require multiple methods of internal and external communication. I also include all forms of illumination (e.g., flashlights, headlamp, chemical lights) in this compartment, although some are stored outside of the main communications' compartment, in separate pouches and sheaths.

- Smartphone
- Extra smartphone battery
- BaoFeng two-way radio
- Monocular
- Chemical lights
- LED flashlight
- LED headlamp
- Mini whistle
- GPS
- Laser pointer
- 22-channel FRS/GMRS two-way radio
- AM/FM digital weather-alert pocket radio
- Orion orange-/red-smoke signal
- Orion Pocket Rocket (4-pack) signal kit
- Rechargeable batteries (to be used in conjunction with my foldable solar panel)
- Compact, portable, external-battery charger USB (2000mAh minimum) for charging batteries/devices when sunlight is not available

Water

The human body cannot survive without water for more than 72 hours, so this may be the most important compartment of the BOB. The water compartment is used for the purification and storage of water. I wanted to have multiple ways of storing drinking water and multiple methods of purifying water in an emergency situation, since it is fairly safe to assume that 1/3 of my preparedness will not work (due to loss or failure). Boiling water in one of the metal containers in the BOB is always an option for purification, but I have added the capabilities of a water-filtration straw and purification tablets as a backup (see "SAS Survival Pouch").

- Bottled water
- Mini water-filter (Sawyer)
- Stainless-steel, wide-mouth bottle
- Hydration bladder (3L)
- Sea to Summit Folding Bucket

Fire

Having multiple fire capabilities is an extremely important aspect of a bug-out bag. A common approach is to have a minimum of three different ways to make a fire. The three methods I chose were a fire steel, BIC lighter(s), and waterproof matches. I chose to use the very popular Wetfire-fire-starting tinder, although the petroleum-based Bag Balm (see "Hygiene") could also be used with fire-starting tinder.

- BIC lighter(s)
- Stormproof matches
- Fire steel

- Wetfire fire starting tinder/cotton balls saturated in petroleum jelly
- Potassium permanganate (KMnO4) and glycerin, when mixed together, will cause a chemical reaction within a few seconds. Eventually the mixtures will produce a white smoke, followed by a bright burst of flame. Glycerin is most commonly used for this purpose, but antifreeze will also do the trick. Antifreeze seems to create a reaction that is a little more violent. Just remember, a little bit goes a long way.

Ideally, potassium permanganate should be stored in a nonreactive container, such as plastic, glass, ceramic, or stainless steel and kept at a temperature <150 degrees. Keep it separate from anything combustible/volatile. Most plastic bottles and non-coated caps should be fine.

Potassium permanganate may be one of the most useful survival chemicals, as it has a multitude of uses, some of which follow.

- Purifying water
- Creating an antiseptic solution
- As an anti-fungal treatment for the hands and feet
- As a cholera disinfectant
- Treating canker sores
- Marking snow as an emergency signal
- General disinfectant agent

Potassium permanganate is not a perfect option for any of the above listed purposes. If other more conventional options are available, use them first. What it does do is offer another alternative should you find yourself with it as your only resource.

Cooking

Long-distance backpackers have developed useful strategies for choosing the best ultralight cooking gear for their cooking compartment. While many of the items are more expensive than other non-ultralight gear, the quality and lightweight materials help justify the initial expense. These items allow for a comfortable, flexible cooking environment, fuel savings, and flavor options.

- Spice Missile (for salt, herbs, or spices)
- Mini spatula
- N-rit towel
- Sea To Summit collapsible bowl
- Sea To Summit Delta InsulMug
- Snow Peak Giga Power stove
- Snow Peak Giga Power fuel canister
- Titanium spork
- Snow Peak titanium trek (700ml pot)
- Pot cozy (check-out YouTube videos to construct your own)
- Sponge

Hygiene

The hygiene compartment is a travel bathroom kit that will not only maintain cleanliness, but also boost morale. Most people feel better about themselves after taking a shower, brushing their teeth, and putting on some clean clothes. The items selected for this compartment meet my minimal sanitary needs and are in travel size when available.

- Bag Balm
- Chap stick
- Deodorant
- Floss
- Hand sanitizer
- Insect repellent
- Kotex super plus tampons
- Disposable razor
- Nail clippers
- Q-tips
- Soap
- Toilet paper
- Toothbrush
- Toothpaste
- Travel laundry detergent packets or soap leaves/sheets
- U-Dig-It stainless-steel hand shovel
- Wet Ones singles
- Extra pair of glasses/contacts and solution

Tools

The tools compartment is designed to provide the basic tools necessary in an urban emergency. Many of the tools listed would be useless in a rural environment, just like the 4-way sillcock lawn faucet key, but highly valuable in an urban environment. If weight ever becomes an issue with this bug-out bag, some of the items included in this list could be left out or carried in your vehicle.

- 550 paracord (50 ft.)
- Bank line (at least 100 lb. tensile strength)
- Gorilla duct tape
- Electrical tape
- Fresnel lens
- General 4-in-1, mini precision screwdriver

- Husky storage bag
- Jones sillcock 4-way lawn faucet key
- Full-tang, fixed-blade knife
- Stainless steel scissors
- Non-contact voltage tester
- Minibolt cutter
- Leatherman charge with black-oxide coating
- Leatherman bit kit
- Mini Gorilla super glue
- Electrical connectors (misc.)
- Nails (misc.)
- Razor blades
- Res-Q-Me emergency-rescue escape tool
- Sharpie marker
- Pocket Pal multi-function knife sharpener
- Stanley 10-in. mini-hack light-duty utility saw
- Sven saw (15 in.)
- Dead On tools annihilator wrecking bar (14 in.)
- Travel-size sewing kit
- Zip ties (various sizes)
- Rubber tubing (36 in.) for siphoning fuel/hard to reach water sources

Clothing

The clothes compartment provides some of the basic clothing items needed for various weather conditions (hot, cold, and rain). While having more clothes would be ideal, the following list is minimalistic in order to save valuable pack space. I try to use clothes that are popular with ultralight backpackers. These are clothes that are ultralight, quick drying, and compress well for packing (avoid cotton.)

- Bandana
- ExOfficio give-n-go boxer briefs
- Travel umbrella
- Ultra-light rain jacket
- Beanie and boonie/hat
- Long-underwear bottoms
- Short-sleeve shirt
- Long-sleeve shirt
- Non-cotton pants (zips off as shorts)
- Balaclava
- Wool socks
- Knee pads
- Work gloves
- Sturdy pair of boots/hiking shoes
- Mosquito head net

Personal

The personal compartment contains various items, including office supplies, entertainment, electronics, snacks, intel, navigation, and documentation. The majority of these items are stored in the numerous pockets in the front compartment of the backpack; however, there are a few that are stored in the main compartment of the backpack as well.

- PDF books, bug-out library (BOL)
- Compass
- Small digital camera
- Deck of cards
- Dice
- Disaster-plan printout
- Goal Zero guide 10 adventure kit (solar panel, lithium battery charger, etc.)
- USB car charger
- 8 GB USB flash drive

- Micro SD card (with adapter)
- Goal Zero Medusa USB universal adapter
- Topo and road maps of your area
- Clear anti-fog safety goggles
- Printout of important phone numbers (family, emergency, etc.)
- SanDisk Sansa Clip+ 4 GB MP3 Player
- *SAS Survival Guide* (Mini version)
- Pocket *Bible*

Money/Barter

Use the most hidden compartment of your bug-out back to conceal and carry $500 in cash—especially in $1 bills. Include a few items for bartering (in the case that paper currency is no longer valuable). Cash will be king when the plastic cards no longer work.

- $500 cash—multiple denominations
- Silver American Eagle x4
- Quarters
- BIC lighters

Weapons

The choice of weapons is heavily weighted by the laws of your city and state. After a collapse, there will be no rule of law. I would recommend a hand gun and four loaded magazines, with more ammo in your vehicle. (Train so that you know how to use a firearm safely and effectively.) I would suggest lethal and non-lethal options.

- Handgun
- 4 magazines loaded, extra ammo in trunk of car

- CLP cleaning oil
- Cleaning patches
- Pepper spray/mace/bear spray
- Expandable baton
- Slingshot/ball bearings
- Assisted opening knife

Baby/Children Supplies

This is the last on the list since not every bug-out situation has a baby/child involved. If you have a baby or child, the items listed below should be top priority, along with making potable water, being able to create fire, and having a shelter.

- Diapers
- Wet wipes
- Baby wash/soap
- Multiple changes of clothes/socks/shoes
- Bibs
- Blankets
- Baby carrier/wrap/sling
- Bottles
- Dish Soap
- Bottle Brush
- Formula (breast is best, though)/baby food
- Water
- Diaper-rash cream/anti-fungal ointment
- Lavender oil
- Pacifiers
- Thermometer
- Bulb syringe (hospital-grade ONLY)
- NoseFrida
- Infant grooming/manicure kit
- Medications (prescription, infant Tylenol/Motrin, teething gel, etc.)
- Ziploc bags

- Coloring book pages/crayons
- Small stuffed animal/doll/toys
- Bedtime story book
- Small electronic game

Urban EDC Altoids Tin

A mini survival kit is a small survival kit consisting of the most essential outdoor survival tools and supplies that are the hardest to improvise or replace. These kits may be referred to as BOATs or bug-out Altoids tins. A mini survival kit is intended to be carried on your person at all times, be appropriate to all environments, and be a comprehensive kit without being too large. Many items included in such a kit are difficult, if not impossible, to manufacture or obtain in real-world survival situations.

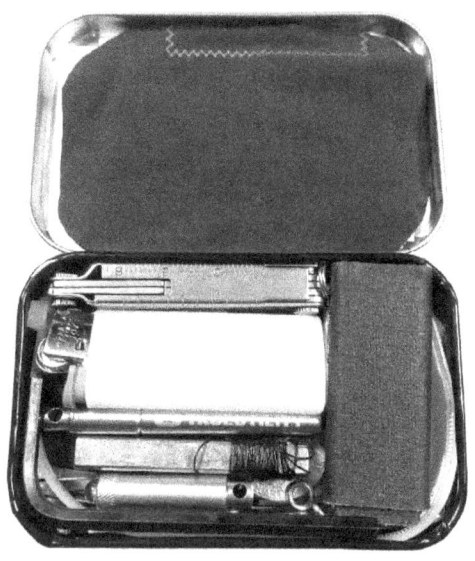

My urban EDC Altoids tin is not designed as a standard survival tin. While items fitting the previously mentioned description would be extremely beneficial in an outdoor emergency, the majority of items have little use for EDC (every day carry) purposes in an urban environment. Instead of carrying a bunch of items that I would most likely never use on a daily basis, I redesigned my kit for convenience of use and practicality in an urban environment. This would be an extremely poor kit to carry in the Amazon jungle, but highly beneficial to have at work, home, for out-of-town travel, and during errands in an urban environment.

The suggested list of items is more than will fit into the tin, but with a little Tetris skill, you can get most of the items in. Just decide what you think
you will use most often, then adjust accordingly as you use it.

- Altoids tin
- Titanium whistle (100+ dB)
- Titanium, keychain-size pry bar
- BIC lighter (mini)
- Emergency phone numbers
- Family photo
- Gaffers tape (14 in.), wrapped around paper clip and/or safety pin
- iGo KeyJuice charger for smartphones
- USB flash drive (8 GB micro)
- True Utility nanolite
- True Utility SlimClips nail clippers
- True Utility Telepen telescopic pen
- 1 sheet of 3x5 Rite In The Rain paper
- 1 Band-Aid
- 2 stamps

- Uncle Bill's sliver gripper tweezers
- Spyderco Bug SS micro-size folding knife
- Leatherman Micra multi-tool
- Lock-pick tools
- Universal handcuff key
- Quarters
- $20 bill
- Razor blade
- Kevlar thread
- Sewing needle
- Safety pins
- Zip ties
- Rx meds/pain pills/daily supplements (individually wrapped in foil)
- Water-purification tablets
- Ranger bands (to keep tin securely closed)

SUMA Container

Another option for an urban EDC is the SUMA container by SOLKOA Survival Systems. It is ultralight and virtually indestructible, machined from a solid block of aircraft grade 6061 aluminum. This aluminum is four times lighter than stainless steel and half the weight of titanium. The container cover includes a rubber gasket to keep out dirt and moisture, and it's secured very simply by heavy-duty Velcro straps. The SUMA large-size container dimensions are: (inside) 4 3/4" x 2 7/8" x 1 3/8" and (outside) 5 1/8" x 3 1/4" x 1 7/8". It is currently being used by Navy Seal Team 6 as their compact survival-kit container. Let that fact sink in for a second! The Altoids tin is a good, low-budget EDC container for around $1.60--but they are intended for mints (I have broken a few). The size is pocket perfection, but a SUMA container will give you a little more room and a million times more protection for your gear—but with a very hefty price tag of $69.95. This may seem like an exorbitantly priced container, but you have to weigh the investment against the items that you would like to carry—are your mini survival items worth $5 or $500.

With the SUMA container you can add:

- A Fisher Space refill pen
- 4 sheets of folded 3x5 Rite In The Rain paper
- Foldable Whirl-Pak 1L bags (for emergency water collection, purification, and storage)
- 2x3 star-flash signal mirror
- Heavy-duty foil
- Larger Leatherman with bits
- Hex keys
- Larger LED flashlight
- Cyalume chemlight lightstick (1.5 in.)

- Fresnel lens magnifier
- Hacksaw blade (cut to fit)
- Set of disposable contact lenses
- Re-rolled and flattened Gorilla tape
- Steri-Strips
- Trauma dressing
- Slide-top tin container(s) for pills
- Antibiotics (veterinarian if you can't get Rx).
- 550 paracord (as much as you can stuff inside, or wrap the outside of the container with it)
- Etc.

Summing It Up

At the end of the day, there is no perfect survival bag. Even my own bags change and evolve when my needs, thoughts, wants, and tastes change. An incomplete and imperfect bag is better than no bag at all. For me, the peace of mind in knowing that it's ready to grab if needed is reason enough for me to have taken the time, effort, and money to have built it.

4
H2O

Water, apart from shelter, will become the most immediate need in a survival situation. Potable water is a vital resource. Depending on your level of activity and what the ambient temperature is outside, you can live for about 3 days, albeit miserable ones, without water. Prolonged activity without proper hydration, coupled with malnutrition, will quickly lower your chances of survival. Finding ways to maintain a source of clean drinking water will be essential for both short- and long-term preparedness. It should tell you how important water is if FEMA distributes it at every major disaster. Water is life. Just one day without this precious fluid will leave you feeling the definite effects of dehydration.

Make sure you are familiar with water sources in your current area, as well as areas you may plan to travel through. Studying Google Earth and topographical maps is always a good idea; this will help you find water while on the move. As with other areas of emergency preparedness, make sure to have a backup plan. Local water sources can change with time, especially due to seasonal fluctuations and the amount of rainfall/snowfall. Another important aspect to finding water is to know the lay of the land. Learning the elevation gradients and thinking about which way the water should travel during a rainstorm can be another way to locate a water source. For the scope of this book, we will assume that a source has been located.

You do not want to wait until you are thirsty to begin gathering water, as the urge to drink directly from a contaminated source may become impossible to bear. If you develop a waterborne illness, this will further dehydrate you, worsening your situation.

Remember that almost all purification methods will remove the biological pathogens, but not the chemical pollutants, so source your water very carefully.

How to Get Emergency Drinking Water from a Water Heater

A typical home water heater can provide between 30 and 60 gallons of clean drinking water during a disaster. Hurricanes, floods, earthquakes, and other power outages may prevent you from having many things, but clean drinking water should not be one of them. To reclaim some clean drinking water from you water heater, and to tap your inner MacGyver, this is what you'll need to do.

1. **Turn off the electricity or gas to the water heater.** Turn off the circuit breaker for electric water heaters or close the gas valve for natural gas and propane types. If the power is still on when the tank is empty, your tank will almost certainly sustain significant damage. Most electric water heaters in residential applications are 208/240 volts, and supplied by a double-pole circuit breaker or two fuses rated at 30 amps.

   • Some gas valves have a thermostatic control knob facing forward. The "Off - Pilot - On" gas supply knob is located on the top, between the red interlock button the black "push-button" ignitor. Simply rotate the top knob from the "On" to the "Off" position to stop the flow of gas to the burner.
   • Some electric-reliant heaters have double-pole 30 amp circuit breakers. Switch the circuit breaker from the "On" position to the "Off." Once off, there is no danger of damaging the heating elements.

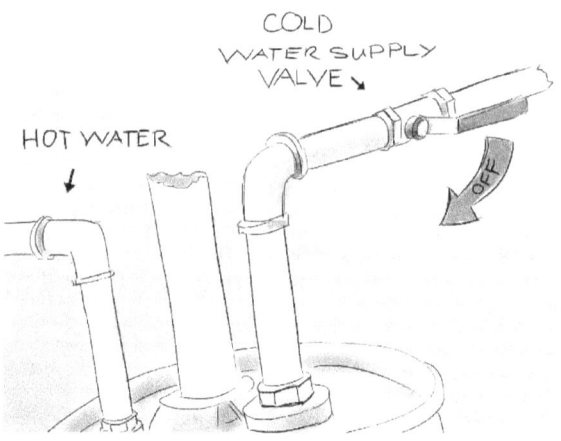

COLD
WATER SUPPLY
VALVE

HOT WATER

OFF

2. **Preserve the cleanliness of the water in the tank by closing the supply valve to the tank.** When water service is restored, the water department will be pumping water that could be contaminated. This will be fine to use for flushing toilets and for cooking, but not for drinking.

- Determine whether you're dealing with a ball valve or a gate valve. Unlike a traditional gate valve's handle, which needs to be turned completely several times in order to shut off, a ball valve handle is rotated just a 1/4 turn between full on and off positions.
- If older, traditional gate valves were installed instead, bear in mind that the color of the handle does not guarantee an association with the temperature of the water in the pipe.

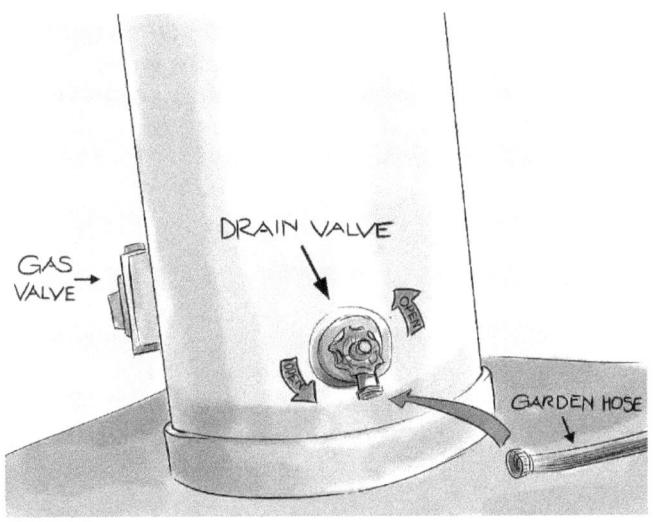

GAS VALVE

DRAIN VALVE

GARDEN HOSE

3. **Find the valve at the bottom of the tank for draining**. This is where your clean drinking water will come from. Many water heater valves have a connector for hooking up a garden hose to the drain valve. A short 3 foot (0.9 m) length of garden hose will make the collection of the water easier. A washing machine's supply hose is the perfect length and is available in many homes. Connect the hose and open the valve briefly to flush any debris that may have collected in the valve. Make sure the drain, hose, and container are clean before using them.

- Threads are usually provided to connect an ordinary garden hose (or washer supply hose). Some gate valves do not have a traditional handle, but rather a slot at the end of the stem where a handle would normally attach.

The slot allows for operation with a screwdriver, or coin. Work this valve gently, as these valves are seldom used more than once or twice per year under normal service conditions, and could be damaged if forced.

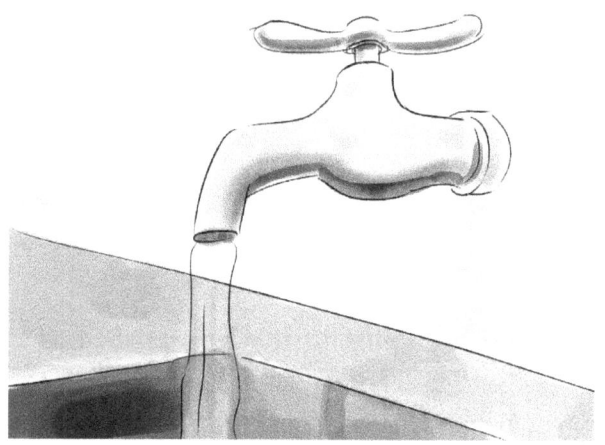

4. **Turn on the hot water from any tap in the house.** In order for water to be drained from the tank, you must allow air to get into it. This is easy to do by opening any hot water tap in the building such as the kitchen or bathroom sink. When either faucet is open, a sucking sound may be heard whenever water is drawn from the water heater's drain valve, and is normal.

5. **Remove any sediment that has collected at the bottom of the water heater.** Water heaters are notorious for trapping sediments. The heavier-than-water sediment sinks and collects at the bottom of the tank because hot water is drawn from the top of the tank, rather than the bottom. If you have sediment in the drinking water let it stand for a period of time to let it settle to the bottom of container.

- Typical mineral sediment that has settled in the hot water is usually harmless, but if your heater has an aluminum anode, there may be a lot of jelly-like aluminum corrosion byproduct on the tank bottom.

- Many people mistakenly believe that the tank is made of glass (or another inert substance). It is not. The inside of the tank will likely be lined with glass to prevent corrosion, since corrosion is the leading cause of water heater failure. There is no danger cooking or consuming water that has been contained in a water heater.

- Although water from a water heater is considered safe to drink, consider purifying or filtering it before drinking. Although it's probably fine to drink water from the heater during an emergency, it's best to be on the safe side. You can purify water by boiling it or using iodine or bleach in very small quantities. You can filter water in an emergency by layering filtering agents on top of each other.

Swimming Pools

The National Swimming Pool Foundation estimates that there are 10-million swimming pools in the United States. Approximately six million are in-ground pools while four million are above ground.

The average in ground pool contains 20,000 gal of water, while the average above ground pool holds 10,000 gal. If you do the math, you will find this equates to billions of gallons of water available during a crisis.

Use the free version of Google Earth to find pools in your neighborhood that could be a potential source of water during a crisis. Obviously, only utilize this resource if the pool owners have abandoned their property or if they have given you permission to use their pool as a water source.

As you are probably already aware, pool water would need to be filtered and purified before drinking.

Other Options for Finding Water

Possible Indoor Sources of Water

- Liquid from canned fruit and vegetables
- Water from the toilet tank (not the toilet bowl)
- Water from melted ice cubes
- Elbow joints of sinks
- Water bed

Possible Outdoor Sources of Water

- Water from rivers, streams, and other moving bodies of water
- Natural springs and artesian wells
- Water from ponds, dams, and lakes
- Residential and public pools
- Water from a rainwater-collection system
- Rolled-up garden hose
- Rain gutters
- City water fountains
- Abandoned buildings and homes
- Aquariums
- Zoos

If you don't have a supply of emergency drinking water, you might have to get creative in order to find clean water, as stated in previous pages. You should definitely store extra water in your home, in your car, and keep water bottles in your grab-and-go bag. This is the most convenient way to ensure survival. At the first sign of impending doom, fill your bathtubs, sinks, pots, and any other large containers that can store water. Even if you have water already stored, you will always want more.

Bodies of Water

Bodies of water are almost always contaminated. When you're in back-country, bodies of water are usually lakes, ponds, creeks, streams, or rivers. For us urban dwellers, we are rarely this fortunate, thus, our bodies of water are usually whatever puddles are left over after a hard rain. If no other source of water is available, you may be forced to collect the only water that you can find. Note: Water that is flowing swiftly is cleaner than water in stagnant pools.

Regardless, you will ALWAYS want to filter and purify water from any above ground source.

Ground Water

Rain soaks into the earth and some of it makes its way down to the water table. The earth is an excellent water filter. If the water table is 100 ft. or more beneath the surface, then the water there is usually safe without any treatment. Note: If purchasing/renting a home, inquire about wells on the property, but not only do you need to be sure to keep your well adequately protected from outside contaminants, but you need to also correctly test for these contaminants as well.

Generally, private-water supplies should be tested for nitrate and bacterial contamination annually. Otherwise, drinking water should be tested if:

- You notice a change in your water quality.
- People using the water suffer from an illness which may be waterborne.
- There is a flood or large storm that may have carried contaminants to your wellhead.
- Maintenance work is done on the well.
- A pregnant woman, a woman anticipating pregnancy, or an infant under the age of six months becomes a water user.

It is best to do coliform bacteria tests in the spring during wet weather. This is when bacteria are most likely to be found because runoff and excess soil moisture can carry contaminants into shallow groundwater sources or through well defects. Testing during dry weather or when the ground is frozen may not indicate the presence of bacteria because they are likely to be at lower concentrations under these conditions.

Test for other substances when specific contamination is suspected. This might be the result of a spill or backflow, use of harmful products in close proximity to the well, or other similar events. Any noticeable change in water taste, color, or smell signals the need for testing.
Even if you do currently have good water quality, routine testing is a smart idea because it establishes a water-quality record. With a water-quality record, if a contaminant problem develops in the future, it will be easier to correlate to the cause.

Don't fail to prepare on the other end of the spectrum as well. What if your electrically-powered well pump should fail due to a power outage? All the testing in the world isn't going to be of any good to you if you can't even pump the water out of the ground. Invest in a hand-operated pump or solar pump. Either of these choices will give you some peace of mind; just make sure, however, to do proper research before making a purchase, as either option can be highly expensive. You want something that is easy to use, affordable, and is quality made, as there is no point in having a back-up plan if it doesn't work adequately when you need it most.

How to Go About Getting Your Water Tested
Whether your drinking water comes from a public water supply (city water) or private well and/or spring, each drinking water source may be at risk for contamination and you need to know what those contaminants are and how you might protect your family from the risks associated with the contamination.

You may be thinking that this is all overkill, but do you want to find out the hard way, in a collapse, that your go to, bug-out-location's well water is not drinkable? How about that natural spring that you are counting on? If it is surface water percolating underground from a farm, pesticides, herbicides, and harmful bacteria from animal waste could be fed into the spring water.

Private wells are primarily unregulated (although a few states are beginning to regulate), so it is up to the homeowner to make sure the water coming from their well is safe for consumption. Most wells are tested at some point in time, but more than likely that testing was only for bacteria. While bacteria pose an immediate health risk, there are other contaminants that lurk in ground water that can cause illness when exposed to small amounts over a long period of time—arsenic and uranium being two good examples.

Public water suppliers (city water) are responsible for testing the water quality as it leaves the water treatment facility and travels potentially miles of pipes throughout the distribution system to your water meter. Thus, your home's interior plumbing is unaccounted for and may be causing lead contamination, depending on the age of your house.

Never have someone who sells water-treatment or water-filtration equipment come into your home to test your water. You should get an independent test from a laboratory, health department, local university, your municipal water provider, or even the local pool-supply company (who will usually test for free).

Yes, you can certainly purchase a do-it-yourself, inexpensive, water-purity test kit from somewhere like Amazon or your local hardware store, but remember that these are going to be basic kits that are not necessarily going to be as accurate or give you the same detailed information as what you are going to get from a professional. With that said, these test kits are easy to use and the results are easily interpretable. For the test itself, you'll dip test strips into your water. Your kit will come with a chart that will help you read the test strips and determine what is in your water. Not only will you be able to see what kind of contaminates may be in your water, you will also be able to see if they are present in safe or dangerous levels.

Better yet are independent labs, NOT connected with selling you any products. These labs will send you out a test kit with all the bottles needed to perform the test/s that you have selected. You simply fill the bottles according to the sampling instructions you received in your kit and then mail them back to the lab. (You do not want to provide contaminated or otherwise compromised water samples for testing.) There are often comprehensive packages covering a multitude of contaminants. Just remember that when testing for pH, it is important that it be tested as quickly as possible after drawing the sample. The pH can often change over time.

If you do have an in-home sales company come into your private home to test your water, you should NOT rely solely on their results. One quick warning sign is if they test your water and fail to leave you with any written test results. You should question that. Even if they do leave you a copy of the test results, they may not be correct.

Sometimes these salesmen don't upgrade their test kits and chemicals properly. They can add water to tests or do other things to alter results or make your home water look worse. This is not to say that this will happen, but that it *could happen*, as it is a common occurrence. In doing the test, the representative may add tablets or drops of chemicals to your tap water, telling you the water will change color or particles will form if it is contaminated. When your water changes before your eyes, the representative may warn you that the water is polluted and may cause cancer. The best solution, you are told, is to buy the company's water treatment device. You should understand, however, that even spring mineral water would "fail" the company's test. For example, in-home water tests may only check for acidity/alkalinity, water hardness, iron, manganese, and color, but none of these are harmful. Offers to test the tap water in your home for free are almost always part of a sales promotion.

If you are on a municipal supply, you can simply call the number on your water bill and ask for basic water quality information. Compare the city's results with what the salesman told you. If the salesman told you a different hardness number for example, BEWARE, as it should be the same. Often their results are inaccurate or wrong in one fashion or another. However, actual lab results from companies who do not sell water treatment equipment are usually quite accurate and dependable in comparison.

Choosing a Professional Lab to Test Your Water Here are the key things to look for in determining which lab to order your test kit from:

- How many contaminants are being tested? There should be a minimum of 200+ parameters. Double check this for yourself. Don't just go by the total number listed, as some companies will inflate their number of parameters tested by duplicating some parameter names or by listing a compound as one contaminant and then list that compound's components as separate contaminants. When an on-line marketing company plays the numbers game, they think you will only look at their parameter count and not check to see if it is accurate.
- Does the company you are ordering your test kit from actually own the lab that will be doing the testing or are they subcontracting the work out and are essentially marketing companies?
- Is the lab utilizing EPA testing methods?
- Does the test kit you order include a postage-paid, return mailing label included in the cost of the test? Some marketing companies will try to trick you into thinking that you are getting a "discount" and then recover it by charging you for "return shipping."
- How many years has this company been in business? What kind of experience does this company have?
- What kind of credentials do those performing the testing have? Are they university-educated professionals or unqualified personnel using test strips or colorimetric kits?

- To find out where you can get a list of state-certified laboratories, call the EPA's Safe Water Drinking Hotline at 1-800-426-4791.

Springs

Although spring water is really surface water, it still originates from groundwater. A spring is a place where water naturally flows out of the ground. This comes from the German word springer, which means "to leap from the ground."

As a side note, when you see your water bottle being advertised as "natural spring water," you may want to be skeptical about that "natural spring" source, because springs are not common enough on Earth to support the enormous bottled-water industry. In fact, while they are an important part of both the water cycle and the ecosystems they're found in, they're actually somewhat rare. Before you spend your money on bottled water, you should know that at least 25% of bottled waters come from municipal sources, so do your homework before stocking up on it. In some regions of the country, where city tap water is of excellent quality and bottled water is only marginal, you might actually do worse with stuff from the supermarket. Some marketing claims for bottled water are strictly regulated, and others are meaningless: glacier, natural, organic, and pure.

"When it comes to spring water quality, it's a tricky subject," according to Rob Blair, a geologist who monitors ground water for the Kentucky Division of Water. "You see a lot of variation in quality. You can pull a sample one day, and it will be clean. Go back tomorrow and it could be the most contaminated water you've ever seen."

Although springs can be a good source of water, they may not provide enough water throughout the year to be a reliable supply. Many springs are fed by water that is fairly close to the soil surface, so that during periods of drought there may not be enough water in these areas to keep the spring flowing at a sufficient rate.

With all of that being said, there is a very handy website called FindaSpring.com. This is a community- and user-created database of natural springs around the world. In fact, their website encourages others to share their knowledge of local springs that are not already listed on their map or in their database.

Their disclaimer informs users to independently test all spring water before making the decision to consume it. This website is simply a source for locating springs and does not validate water safety.

How to Turn Salt Water into Drinking Water

Desalination is the process of removing salt from saltwater. Humans cannot safely drink salinated water. All simple methods for removing the salt from water follow a basic principle: evaporation and collection. This section addresses several methods that can be used to boil salty water and collect freshwater from the steam or condensation, ranging from a stove-top method, a survival method, and a solar method.

Using a Pot and Stove

1. **Get a large pot with a lid and an empty drinking cup.** The glass should be big enough to hold a fair amount of fresh water.

   - Make sure the glass is short enough that you can still put the lid on the pot.
   - A Pyrex or metal cup is safest, as certain types of glass will explode when exposed to heat. Plastic may melt or deform.
   - Make sure the pot and lid are suitable for using on a standard stove or outdoor, camp-type stove.

2. **Slowly pour some salt water into the pot**. Do not overfill.

- Stop well before the water level has reached the mouth of the glass to ensure that no salt water splashes into the glass while boiling, otherwise, your newly made fresh water will be contaminated.

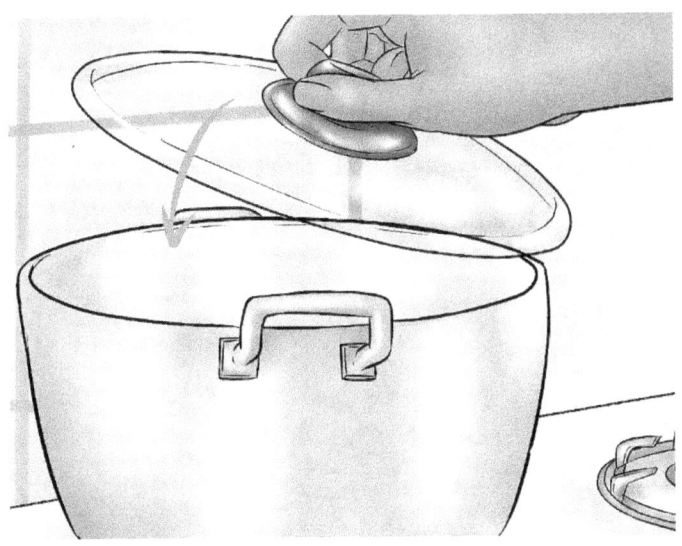

3. **Place the pot cover upside down on the pot.** This will allow the water vapor, as it condenses, to drip into the drinking glass.

- Position the pot lid so the highest point or handle is facing down directly above the glass.
- Make sure the pot lid is providing a good seal along the edges of the pot. Without a good seal, a lot of the steam will escape and diminish the supply of fresh-water vapor.

4. **Bring the water to a slow boil over low heat.**

- A violent, full boil can contaminate the drinking water by splashing into the glass.
- Too much heat can cause a glass to break.
- If the water is boiling quickly and violently, the glass may shift away from the center of the pot and the handle of the pot lid.

5. **Watch the pot as the water condenses.**
   When water boils, it becomes pure vapor, leaving behind anything that was dissolved in it.

   - As the water becomes vapor, it condenses in the air as steam and on the cover's surface as water droplets.
   - The droplets then run down to the lowest point (the handle) and drip right into the glass.
   - This will probably take 20 minutes or more.

6. **Wait until the glass of water cools down before drinking from it**.

  • There may be a small amount of salt water left in the pot, so be very careful not to splash any salt water into your fresh water when removing the glass.
  • Be careful as you remove the glass so you don't get burnt. Use an oven mitt or pot holder to take it out.

Using Solar Desalination

1. **Collect salt water in a bowl or container.** Make sure you don't fill it up all the way.

   - You will need some space at the top of the bowl so that the salt water doesn't splash into your fresh water receptacle.
   - Make sure your bowl or container is watertight. If it is leaking, your salt water will drain away before it can form steam to condense as fresh water.
   - Make sure you have plenty of sunlight as this method takes several hours.

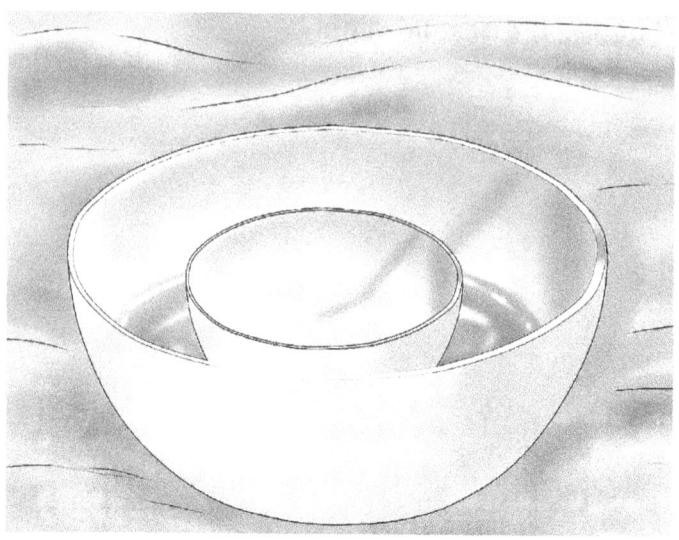

2. **Place a cup or smaller container in the center very cautiously**.

- If you do this quickly, you might get some salt water splash into your cup. This will contaminate your fresh water as you collect it.
- Make sure the lip of the glass remains above water.
- You might need to weight it down with a rock to prevent it from sliding around.

3. **Cover the bowl with plastic wrap.** Make
   sure the wrap isn't too loose or too tight.

   • Be sure that the plastic wrap has a tight
     seal on the rim of the salt-water bowl.
   • If there are any tears in the plastic
     wrap, steam or fresh water vapor might
     escape, this is why you will want to use
     a sturdy brand of plastic wrap.

4. **Place a rock or weight in the center of the plastic wrap**. Do this just above the cup or container in the center of the bowl.

- This will cause the plastic wrap to dip in the center, allowing fresh water to drip into your cup.
- Make sure your rock or weight isn't too heavy or it will tear the plastic wrap.
- Make sure the cup is in the center of the bowl before continuing.

5. **Place the salt water bowl in direct sunlight**. This will heat the water and cause condensation to form on the plastic wrap.

- As condensation forms, fresh water droplets will drip from the plastic wrap into the cup.
- This will allow you to slowly collect fresh water.
- This method takes several hours, so be patient.
- After you have enough fresh water in your cup, you can drink it safely. It is now completely desalinated.
- Solar methods take a longer period of time and might not be adequate for making lots of fresh water quickly.

Water-Storage Options

Bottled Water
The International Bottled Water Association (IBWA) advises consumers to store bottled water at room temperature or cooler, out of direct sunlight and away from solvents and chemicals such as gasoline, paint thinners, household cleaners, and dry-cleaning chemicals.

First, when water (bottled water or tap water) is exposed to extended periods of direct sunlight or heat sources, algae or mold may infrequently develop. Although this is not a general concern for public heath, to enjoy the freshest, cleanest water possible, storing water in a cool place out of direct sunlight will help assure that.

Second, bottled water and other beverages are packaged in sanitary and highly protective, sealed, plastic containers that maintain the quality and freshness of the product. However, plastic containers—whether used for bottled water or other beverages—are slightly permeable, which may allow ambient air gases, such as vapors from household solvents, petroleum-based fuels, and other chemicals to affect the taste and odor. Proper storage will help ensure product quality.

Consumers also ask about expiration dates printed on some bottles and whether bottled water has a limited shelf life. The U.S. Food and Drug Administration (FDA), which regulates bottled water as a packaged food product, has determined that there is no limit to the shelf life of bottled water. Since it is packaged under sanitary, good-manufacturing processes, is in a sanitary, sealed container, and does not contain substances (such as sugars and proteins) typically associated with food spoilage, bottled water can be stored for extended periods of time without concern. In addition, only one state (New Jersey) has ever required expiration dating for bottled water. However, the New Jersey state legislature repealed the 2-year-expiration-date law several years ago, noting that there was no scientific evidence to support such a requirement.

Some companies place date-based lot codes on bottled water containers, which are typically used to assist in managing stock rotation at distribution and retail points.

As you can see, bottled water is an excellent choice for emergency water storage. Not only is it safe, but very convenient. How easy is it to grab a flat of water every time you are at Costco for a few bucks? What's nice too is that there are multiple sizes of bottled water, depending on your preference, ranging from 8 oz. to 1.5 L. Bottled water also comes in jugs if you would prefer, usually in the 1 gal size, but there are also 2.5 gal jugs that have a spigot for ease of use. If you want to go the easiest route, although not the most cost effective, contact a bottled-water delivery service. Although they can certainly deliver the smaller sizes as listed above, most folks take advantage of the larger sizes for home and at work, such as the 3 gal or 5 gal sizes, which are normally used in conjunction with a water dispenser.

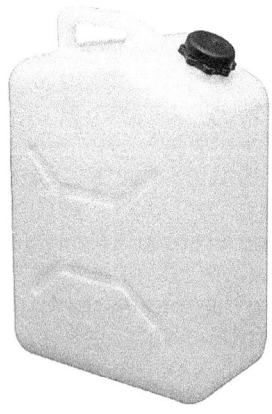

5-7 Gal. Containers

These are ideal for daily use or for bugging-out because they are easy to fill, move, and use. Stick with a name brand that says BPA free and has a good seal on the screw-on cap to keep your water fresh and to prevent leaking. 7 gal. is about the most you can have for a container that is considered portable—it weighs nearly 60 lbs. when full.

15-55 Gal. Barrels

These barrels can be purchased inexpensively from food-processing plants or from Craigslist; just make sure that they are food-grade plastic. The prior contents may have leached into the plastic over time, allowing the previous flavors to reintroduce themselves into the water when stored. Although this won't hurt you, who wants that after taste with every sip of water, so before filling, make sure to thoroughly clean any residue from the containers.

275-Gal. IBC Totes

IBC stands for "intermediate bulk container". IBC totes are large tanks that are used to store and transport fluids and other bulk materials. IBC tanks are composed of three primary components: the IBC plastic container, the IBC metal cage, and the container's pallet, which can be made from wood, plastic, or metal. You can purchase them for as little as $65 each from food-processing plants and Craigslist. Just make sure that they are local for pick-up, otherwise the shipping will kill you.

They can be stacked vertically to conserve space, and from what I've read, buried as well. They can be connected to your rain gutter, thus creating an awesome rainwater-collection set-up.

Ways to Treat Water

Pre-Filtering
Unless you want drinking water with leaves, algae, dirt, etc., pre-filtering is recommended, and will extend the life of your water-filtration device, if using one. Pre-filtering large matter can be accomplished by pouring the water through a:

- Bandanna
- T-shirt
- Sock
- Pant leg
- Cheese cloth
- Bath towel
- Screen

The water must then be disinfected by one of the following means:

Boiling
This process is recognized as the safest treatment method. Bring water to a rolling boil for a minimum of 10 minutes. Cover the pot to shorten the time it takes to boil. For every 1000 ft. (305 m) above sea level, add one more minute to the boiling time.

Boiling water removes all chlorine as well as the bacteria. If you don't plan on drinking the water right away, add bleach.

While the boiled water cools, keep it covered with a lid, as airborne bacteria can contaminate it. Anything that is not sterile (like a water storage container) may have bacteria in it. Boiling water only kills the germs in the water, so make sure that the water container that will be used for storing the water has also been decontaminated.

Bleach
In an emergency, think of 1 gal. of Clorox Regular-Bleach) as 3,800 gal. of drinking water. When the tap water stops flowing, bleach isn't just a laundry aid, it's a lifesaver. It's the same in any natural disaster.

As the shock wears off and the days wear on, the biggest demand is for drinking water. Time after time, relief crews hand out free Clorox with simple instructions, "Use it to kill bacteria in your water and you'll have purified water to drink."

Keep an eyedropper taped to your emergency bottle of Clorox, since purifying small amounts of water require only a few drops. Bleach must be fresh for best use and results.

First, let water stand until particles settle. Filter the particles, if necessary, with layers of cloth, coffee filters, or fine paper towels. Pour the clear water into an uncontaminated container and add bleach per the ratio indicated below. Mix well. Wait 30 minutes. Water should have a slight odor of bleach. If not, repeat the dose. Wait another 15 minutes. Sniff again. Remember, all of this will be in vain if you pour your purified water into contaminated containers; therefore, ALWAYS sanitize your water jugs FIRST. In lieu of steamy, hot water for sanitizing dishes, pots, and utensils, use a little bleach instead. Just follow the directions below.

Whether you use bleach in an emergency or for everyday chores, it's always an environmentally sound choice. After its work is done, bleach breaks down to little more than salt and water, which is always acceptable.

Ratio of Regular Strength Bleach to Water for Purification (Use Half as Much for Double Strength Bleach)

2 drops of Clorox Regular-Bleach per qt. of water

8 drops of Clorox Regular-Bleach per gal. of water

1/2 tsp Clorox Regular-Bleach per 5 gal. of water

If water is cloudy, double the recommended dosages of bleach. Use ONLY Clorox Regular-Bleach, without scents, dyes, or additives. To ensure that your bleach is at its fullest strength, rotate or replace your storage bottle at least every 3 months.

Dry Chlorine
Calcium hypochlorite has the added benefit of extended shelf life over household bleach, providing it's kept cool, dry, and in an airtight container. Dry chlorine may be stored up to 10 years with minimal degradation. If you want to keep chlorine in bulk, this is the item to have on hand. It's available at swimming-pool supply stores and many hardware and grocery stores. It also requires less storage space than its liquid counterpart. When purchasing calcium hypochlorite, make sure there are no other active ingredients in it. Calcium hypochlorite is the solid form, with 65-70% strength. Sodium hypo-chlorite is the liquid form.

Using simple precautions make it an excellent choice! Just remember to be VERY cautious when using dry Chlorine: keep it dry, never breathe in the fumes, and always wear gloves while adding it to water.

Iodine
Iodine emerged as a water purifier after WW2, when the U.S. military looked for a replacement to halazone tablets. Iodine was found to be in many ways superior to chlorine in treating small batches of water. Iodine is effective in lower doses and is less sensitive to pH and organic content of water.

Iodine is normally used in doses of 8ppm to treat clear water for a 10-minute-contact time. The effectiveness of this dose has been shown in numerous studies.

Cloudy water needs twice as much iodine or twice as much contact time. In cold water (below 41°F or 5°C), you must double the dose or time. In any case, doubling the treatment time allows you to use half as much iodine.

If no instructions are provided on the container, use 12 drops per gal. of water. If the water is in question, double the amount of iodine. Mix well and allow the water to stand for 30 minutes before using. Iodine is light sensitive, must be stored in a dark bottle, and works best in water over 68°F (21°C).

Sunlight
Solar disinfection is an effective way to disinfect water using only sunlight and a bottle. Filtering the water first will make it clearer so that it will disinfect more quickly.

1. Clean a clear plastic/glass bottle or a plastic bag. Bottles made of polyethylene terephthalate, commonly abbreviated as PET or PETE, plastic work best.

2. Fill the bottle half-full and then shake it for 20 seconds. This will add air bubbles to the water.

3. Then fill the bottle or bag to the top. The air bubbles will help to disinfect the water faster.

4. Place the bottle where there's no shade and where people and animals will not disturb it, such as on the roof of a house. Leave the bottle for at least 6 hours in full sun or for 2 days if the weather is cloudy.

Bio-Filter Water Bottle
This simple filtering system is used worldwide to purify drinking water. While it may not get all pathogens out, it will get out enough that so that you can safely drink the water, allowing your body to destroy the few that manage to get through the filter.

Actually, a bio-filter works almost the same way that a sewage-treatment plant does. The standard for a water-treatment plant is that the water that leaves it must be clean enough to drink. To accomplish this, they use a multi-stage approach to remove anything harmful from the water. Likewise, a bio-filter uses a multi-stage approach to remove impurities and pathogens from the water, so that the water that remains is drinkable. The only difference is you can do it yourself.

This water filter is very easy and quick to make. Most, if not all the materials, can be found in or around your house.

Materials Needed

- Water bottle
- Scissors or knife
- Coffee filter, cotton balls, or fabric
- Sand or charcoal
- Small gravel
- Large gravel or small rocks

- Cup to hold filtered and non-filtered water.

1. Using your scissors or knife, cut off the bottom of the water bottle.

2. Using your knife, scissors, or anything sharp, make a small hole in the center of the cap. Make sure the cap is on tight! In my case, I used a small screwdriver off my multi-tool and easily made a nice hole in the center.

3. Now, stick your coffee filter (or cotton balls or fabric) through the top hole and down by the cap. You may have to cut the size of the coffee filter down to make it fit nicely inside the bottle. Use whatever you have available to push the coffee filter down to the bottom.

4. Now get your sand or crushed charcoal and fill up the bottle about 2 in.

5. Next, add your small gravel. Around 2 in. of gravel should be adequate.

6. Finally, add your large gravel or small rocks. Again, 1-2 in. is enough. Your water filter is now complete! Place/nest the filter on top of your drinking cup and with your other hand, pour the cup of dirty, unfiltered water into the filter.

Watch your dirty water come out clean! Boil the filtered water to completely rid it of all waterborne pathogens!

Enjoy!

Sawyer MINI Water Filter

The Sawyer MINI water filter is the lightest and most versatile personal filtration system on the market. While incredibly small and convenient, this filter was tested to 10 million parts of bacteria and one million parts of protozoa without a single breakthrough, the highest testing level for filtration.

The size, convenience, and performance of the Sawyer MINI filter make it perfect for your pack, your car, and your home. Do not get stuck in a predicament in which the water you have available to you cannot be trusted. This water filter comes with my highest recommendations, especially for the price, along with hundreds of positive feedbacks on *Amazon.com*. The current cost is only $18.99.

- High-performance filter fits in the palm of your hand, weighs 2 oz., and filters up to 100,000 gal. (30 times more than comparable filters)
- Attaches to the included drinking pouch or to standard disposable water bottles and hydration packs, or use the straw to drink directly from your water source
- Removes 7 log (99.99999%) of all bacteria and 6 log (99.9999%) of all protozoa Sawyer's certified, 0.1 absolute micron filters remove bacteria and protozoa at a higher rate than accepted EPA guidelines. This makes it impossible for harmful bacteria, protozoa, or cysts, like E. coli, Giardia, Vibrio cholerae, and Salmonella

Typhi (which cause Cholera and Typhoid) to pass through.

Water: Building Block of Life

Water is the most important nutrient for your body. On average, the human body is 60% water by weight, depending on certain factors such as age, gender, and body weight. The average 70 kg/154 lb. man is made up of 42 L/11 gal. of water, while the average 55-kg/121 lb. adult female is made up of 27.5/7.2 gal. of water. Within the body, water is divided between two major fluid compartments: 40–50% of total body water is contained within the cells, called intracellular fluid; 50–60% is outside the cells (extracellular fluid).

So, why is water so important? It performs numerous, important biological functions in the body. First, at the cellular level, it provides structural firmness. Second, water makes up blood, lymph, gastric secretions, and urine. It helps lubricate our joints (synovial fluid), which allows bones to move freely against each other. It also forms blood plasma, which transports oxygen, glucose, and amino acids to active muscle and tissue, while carrying away carbon dioxide and lactic acid. During exercise, muscles produce lactic acid (plus other acids), and too much lactic acid can impair muscle contractility and performance. Third, water helps maintain core-body temperature (thermoregulation). Your body uses water as a cooling mechanism (through sweating) to adequately control its temperature. Even in moderately warm weather, significant amounts of water are lost through sweat. Under more arduous training conditions, it's estimated that sweat losses in endurance athletes exercising in heat and humidity can be nearly 3 L/hr.

Dehydration

Even a mild deficit of water can have a substantial impact on well-being, exercise performance, and attentiveness. Defined, dehydration is the loss of body water and important ions (blood salts like potassium and magnesium). It simply means your body doesn't have as much water and electrolytes as it should have, which interferes with normal body processes.

You don't have to run a marathon to become dehydrated. Each day you lose approximately two to 2–2 ½ (450 to 600 ml) of water just going about your usual activities, so it is important to replace fluid losses throughout the day. Coffee, tea, and sodas are not an ideal choice. These beverages have a diuretic effect (i.e., trigger water loss) and actually increase your daily fluid requirement.

The current RDA of water for adults at rest, under average conditions of environmental exposure, is 1 mL/Kcal of energy expenditure.

For women, this amount would equal 2.2 L/day and for men, 2.9 L/day.

Any individual can become dehydrated from the following conditions:

- Excessive sweating (e.g., endurance exercise, working outdoors, etc.)
- Vomiting and/or diarrhea
- Fever
- Excessive urine output (due to uncontrolled diabetes or diuretic medications).

Infants, children, pregnant and breastfeeding women, those experiencing illness, and elderly adults have increased needs for water.

Infants and children, because of their smaller size and weight, can quickly become dangerously dehydrated if they're experiencing vomiting, diarrhea, fever, and refuse to eat or drink anything.

Elderly adults are another group at risk for dehydration because the thirst desire is reduced as people age. It's imperative that elderly adults (especially those who live in hot climates and/or who don't have air-conditioning) drink plenty of fluids before they become thirsty.

Excessive vomiting and diarrhea (lasting longer than 24 hours) is a cause for concern and is a risk factor for dehydration. Usually, the best way to treat it is to increase fluid intake to replace fluids lost through diarrhea/vomiting. In addition, one can also add a rehydration solution, which can be sipped every 2–3 minutes.

Mild Dehydration

- Dry lips and mouth
- Dry, pasty skin
- Thirst
- Inside of mouth slightly dry
- Low urine output/fewer wet diapers
- Concentrated urine appears dark yellow
- Fatigue
- Insomnia
- Headaches
- Dizziness
- Irritability
- Muscle Cramps
- Constipation

Moderate Dehydration

- Thirst
- Very dry mouth
- Sunken eyes
- Sunken fontanels (the soft spots on an infant's head)
- Tenting (if skin doesn't bounce back readily after it is pinched and lifted slightly)
- Low or no urine output
- Not producing tears

At these signs, children under the age of 12 should see a physician immediately.

Severe Dehydration

- All signs of moderate dehydration
- Rapid and weak pulse
- Cold hands and feet
- Rapid breathing
- Blue lips
- Lethargic, comatose, seizures

Severe dehydration requires immediate hospitalization.

How to Monitor Your Hydration Status

Thirst is a signal that your body needs fluid; however, it's a poor indicator of your body's fluid needs because you can lose 2% of your body weight before you feel thirsty.

A better way to gauge your hydration status is to monitor the output and color of your urine. A well-hydrated individual should void 1,000 to 1,500 mL/day, and urine color should be no darker than a pale yellow color. If your urine is darker, it is a sign you are dehydrated, and you need to increase your fluid intake.

This is why it is imperative to have oral rehydration salts (ORS) readily available. They should really be stored in every medicine cabinet, every home and automobile first-aid kit, and every hidden cache. Since these are powders, shelf-life shouldn't be a concern. There are two notable products that can be ordered online, both having a 4.5 star rating on Amazon.com. Both were created by clinicians, are easy to use, and are fairly affordable. I am talking about Recover ORS and DripDrop. Recover ORS is for children 12 years of age and older and Drip-

Drop is for any age, but especially for children, as this product was designed with a child's picky palate in mind. Both products use no artificial colors, flavorings, or preservatives. Electrolytes help usher water across the intestinal wall into your bloodstream, thus, both products use the golden ratio of ingredients designed for maximum absorption. Either can be taken at the first signs of dehydration, from such things as traveler's diarrhea, food poisoning, stomach flu, fever, diarrhea, vomiting, hangover, and extreme sports.

There are easy alternatives to packaged/commercial ORS. Since the recipes/ingredients are readily available, it shouldn't be hard for you to make your own. There are two standard recipes, consisting of only 3 simple ingredients each: water, salt, sugar (the most common recipe) or water, salt, and cereal. Both recipe descriptions follow with an easy-to-understand pictorial for each.

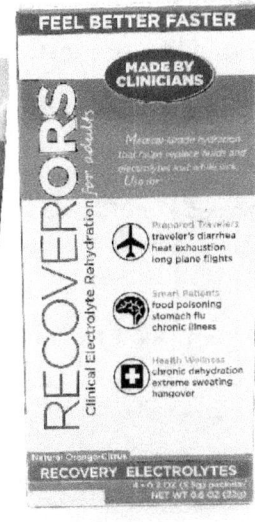
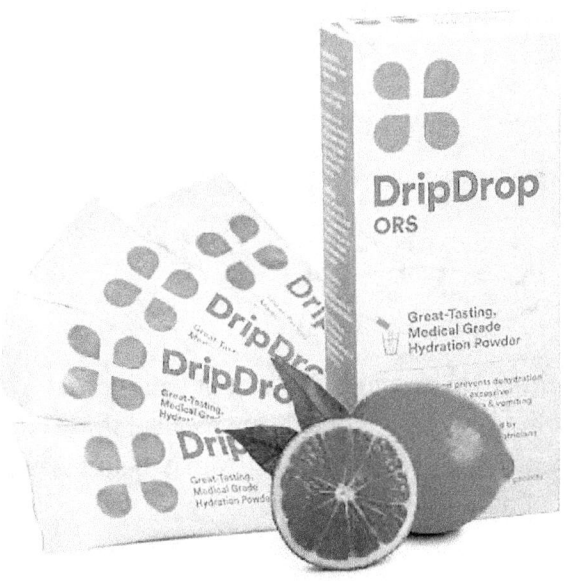

1. WITH SUGAR AND SALT (Raw sugar or molasses can be used instead of sugar)

In 1 liter of clean **WATER** put half of a level teaspoon of **SALT** and 8 level teaspoons of **SUGAR.**

CAUTION: Before adding the sugar, taste the drink and be sure it is less salty than tears.

To either Drink add half a cup of fruit juice, coconut water, or mashed ripe banana, if available. This provides potassium which may help the child accept more food and drink.

2. WITH POWDERED CEREAL AND SALT

(Powdered rice is best. Or use finely ground maize, wheat flour, sorghum, or cooked and mashed potatoes.)

In 1 liter of **WATER**   put half a teaspoon of **SALT**   and 8 heaping teaspoons (or 2 handfuls) of powdered **CEREAL** .

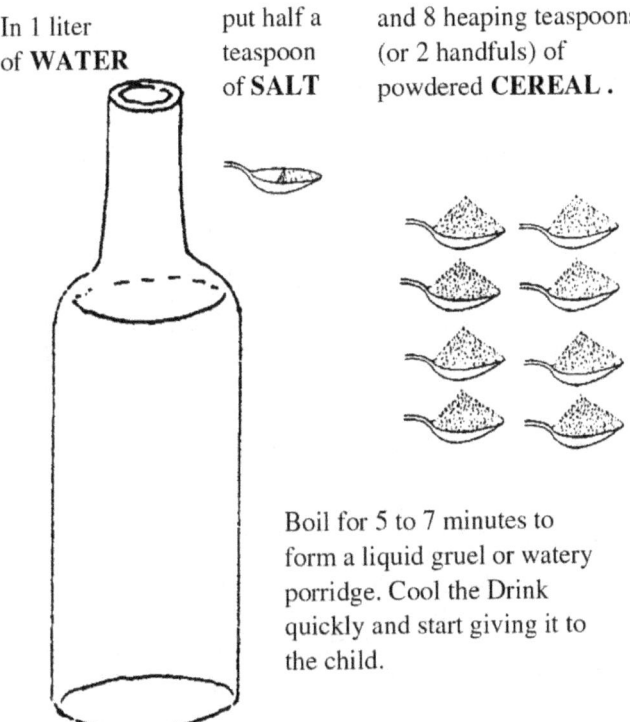

Boil for 5 to 7 minutes to form a liquid gruel or watery porridge. Cool the Drink quickly and start giving it to the child.

CAUTION: Taste the Drink each time before you give it to be sure it is not spoiled. Cereal drinks can spoil in a few hours in hot weather.

5
FOOD

30 Days' Worth of Food

FEMA recommends 3 days' worth of food and water to last most common emergencies, but for a comfortable margin of error, at least 30 days is a better goal to shoot for. If you have a month or more of food stored in your house, you don't have to worry about going out to fight the lines of panicked people who waited until the last-minute to do what you have already done.

Storing food can be complicated and costly, but it is possible to start with a very simple list of items that you can purchase from your local grocery store or from big-box chains like Wal-Mart, Costco, or Sam's Club. I have compiled a simple list of common foods that you can go get today that will allow you to feed a family of 4 for 30 days. If you have more or less people or want to stockpile for longer periods of time, then you can adjust accordingly.

Basic Foods
Although you can shop for any of these items at most grocery stores, I prefer Costco, because I can buy larger quantities at once, thus, saving me time and money. Since I have to go shopping anyway, I might as well enjoy the food samples along the way, as well as the great customer service. Due to the fact that Costco sells in bulk and many food vendors buy from Costco in large amounts, there

will be no questioning gazes from fellow customers or employees.

Rice
First off, buy a 50 lb. bag of rice. This contains 504 servings. This is a pretty safe choice, as most people like rice, even children. It is simple to cook and stores for years if you keep it cool and dry. This bag at Costco runs about $22.

Beans/Legumes
Next, buy a bag of dry beans. You can now check-off the "beans" part of your "beans, bullets, and Band-Aids' list." Although most folks will think of the common pinto bean for this category, Costco carries multiple types of dry beans: black, garbanzo, red, and Mayocoba beans, as well as lentils. Of course, you can buy other varieties of beans and legumes elsewhere. Remember, legumes are among the most versatile and nutritious foods available. Beans/legumes should always be considered a staple, especially when eaten with rice, as this mixture creates a complete protein. You can buy these bags from a range of 20 to 50 lbs., with a price range of approx. $18 to $40, depending on how much you are buying and what type of bean you are choosing.

Canned meat
For canned meat, I recommend tuna or chicken. These are clean meats that can easily be mixed into your rice. You will need approximately 35 cans. Although the most costly out of the bunch, you are buying what your family probably already eats on a regular basis; this will make re-stocking fairly easy. With this meat duo, you are probably looking at $70 for a one months' supply for four.

Canned Vegetables

You will need about 40 cans of vegetables. Choose whatever your family will eat, but try your best to buy a wide variety, as you still want to provide a wide range of nutrition for your family. Expect to pay around a dollar for each regular-sized can, so you will spend approx. $40 for veggies that will last your family one month.

Canned Fruit

Again, choose simple fruits that your family will really eat. Just like with the vegetables, buy approx. 40 regular-sized cans, which will cost you somewhere in the neighborhood of $40. Be careful with the #10 cans, unless freeze-dried, as though you may think you are saving money and stocking-up quickly, what will you do with any leftovers? Assuming you have no refrigeration, what are you going to do with the 21 servings that are left over after your family of four has eaten a serving each from your #10 can? This is why you should always buy in serving sizes that are modest, so that once the meal is complete, there are no leftovers to worry about.

Oatmeal

Good old-fashioned oatmeal is simple to cook and store. A normal container has 30 servings each, so purchase about 4 of these and your family won't starve for breakfast. At $2 each, that's about $8 for a months' worth of breakfast for a family of four. This is a filling, nutritious, easy-to-prepare, and inexpensive meal.

Honey

Honey is a miracle food, really, as it will never go bad. You can use honey in place of sugar to satisfy your sweet tooth. Honey even has medicinal properties and can be used as a flavoring. The most cost-effective way to buy honey is in bulk. If you want to allow each of your family of four to have two tablespoons of honey per day, for 30 days, you should probably buy a gallon of honey. Go to your local farmer's market or to one of your local farms and make sure to buy RAW honey ONLY, that hasn't been filtered, heated, or processed, as this is the only way to get all of the nutrients out of this superfood, which is especially important when compromised during a crisis scenario. You should probably expect a $50 (give or take) price tag or so. If you live in the city and don't have this type of access, then simply order online, as there are a whole host of options, although shipping may add to the initial price tag.

Salt

Table salt, kosher salt, or sea salt will stay as fresh as the day you bought it and remain so throughout the years. Salt will never fail to enhance your meals and as you probably know, sodium is a very important electrolyte, especially during heavy exertion. Of course, there are a wide variety of salts, with varying prices, but probably the best choice would be to go with a sea salt enriched with iodine. This will be about $6, but is well worth it. The chemical composition of sea salt is typically the same as the ions dissolved in seawater. The typical composition by dry weight percent includes: 55.5% chloride; 30.8% sodium; 7.7% sulfate; 3.7% magnesium; 1.2% calcium; 1.1% potassium. Plus, you will have the added benefit of the iodine added as well. With a pinch here and a dash there, you are including very important minerals in your diet.

Vitamins and Minerals

Multivitamins/multi- minerals are good for preventing conditions that arise from severe deficiency, which will likely occur in a crisis-setting without the wide variety of foods that we normally eat on a daily basis. (Well, I guess this isn't necessarily the case, if you eat fast food, junk food, and snack food on a daily basis. Remember, "eat a rainbow.") Granted, the nutrient absorption rate isn't going to be the same as getting that nutrient from a whole food, but you can at least mimic that effect by purchasing a high-quality, whole-food multivitamin/multimineral combination. I know that we all like to save money, but as the old adage goes, "you get what you pay for." Don't buy a synthetic pill that has additives, is cheaply made, has poor absorption, and will give you an upset stomach if taken without a meal. Yes, Centrum will only cost you about $12 for a month's supply for one person, but you practically might as well not even spend your money for the little reward, if any, that your body will get in return. New research is finding out that synthetic vitamins/minerals can actually do more harm than good. For a good quality multivitamin/multi-mineral, you are probably looking at a $30 investment for a month's supply. Now, I know what you are thinking: times that price by four, and you are now at $120 for a one month's supply for your family—wrong! If you buy in bulk, for instance, you are probably looking at $70-$85 in total. Don't forget about the kiddos, if you have any, as you will need to by a children's version as well, which will be less expensive. Make sure to buy online, and shop around, as this will definitely be the least expensive route to take, especially when buying in bulk (which is how the last price quote was determined). Garden of Life and Mega-

Food are reputable brands. I'm sure that there are other great brands, but these are the two that I am familiar with. As a side note, don't fail to rotate your multivitamin/multimineral complex and watch for the expiration date, as potency will be lost past that date, as well as effectiveness. Also, If not stored properly, vitamins will lose their potency even faster. Exposure to heat, light, and air can cause vitamins to degrade more quickly as well. Store the vitamins in their original containers in a cool, dry place. Do not allow the vitamins to be exposed to heat or light.

To Sum It Up

This grocery list will feed the average family of four for 30 days and is a great start to your own food preparations. The meat and supplements were the most expensive part of the bill; with everything included, you are looking at a grand total that comes to $350 (give or take), but this tally, of course, will vary depending on where you live and where/how you shop.

Should you stop there? No, but this is a good starting point. You can certainly expand your horizons by adding to this list in a creative fashion, which will ultimately add variety and nutrition to your table. I would keep all of these items in your pantry, along with your regular groceries, and rotate these to keep the contents fresh.

Once you have mastered the above, I would recommend looking into storing larger quantities in Mylar bags or purchasing freeze-dried foods and some Meals Ready to Eat (MREs).

To make your meals more palatable, you should also store bouillon cubes and spices/dried herbs. Herbs and spices have wonderful health properties that are an added bonus.

Is this gourmet dining? No, but this basic list will keep your family alive.

Long-Term Storage

OK, so I will now assume that you have advanced from your 30-day supplies, maybe having moved-up to 6-month's supplies; but let's pretend that you are REALLY serious about this stuff and want to go all the way. Once you have 6 months of the food you normally eat in the pantry, you should augment your supplies with long-term storage foods. These are foods with a shelf live measured in decades, not years, and they are the perfect "set it and forget it" option for long-term planning. There are several different methods of buying processed foods, or you can do the work yourself and save some money in the long run.

There must be dozens of suppliers of freeze-dried or dehydrated foods on the market. The products, packaging, and processes used to create these options vary somewhat, but the end result is generally the same: this is food that requires no refrigeration (although a cool storage environment is ideal).

It's easy, you essentially purchase kits that have a set number of meals, all individually stored, or in #10 cans. I think that all of the vendors are moving away from #10 cans, though, and going to the stackable, plastic tubs. These not only store all of your food, which comes nicely packaged in Mylar bags, but the buckets can be reused when the food is all gone.

There are many ways to determine the value of each vendor's products before shelling-out thousands of dollars. The only way to do this, however, is to do your research. Once you have settled on a few vendors, start testing some of their products out. Most companies will either sell you a sample pack for a really low price, or they will ship you a small sample for free. For those of you who have never had freeze-dried food before, it's an experience, and I would caution you that while some of these meals are very good, this isn't gourmet eating. You're buying food that will last you for 30 years so that you have something to eat when you're starving. You aren't going to get Ruth's Chris Steak House flavor out of your freeze-dried ground beef, but it will, most certainly, keep you alive.

Build Capacity to Grow Your Own Renewable Food Source

The last category is usually what people wait on until it's too late. It could be that you live in an apartment or have no room to plant a garden. It may be that you have already tried to grow some fruits and veggies, but ended up with a patch full of weeds that would make a Billy goat choke. Regardless of the reason, having the ability to grow your own food is going to be the most important part of your food-security plan. This is going to be the toughest part, because it will actually involve hard work, and more importantly, your time and energy.

As far as I know, you can't go out and buy a garden in a can. Yes, there are a lot of places that sell survival seed banks/vaults. Yes, this is definitely something to consider if you have a garden already, but you should not expect to walk out your back door after the grid has gone down and have a Jack in the Beanstalk miracle overnight. Gardening requires a lot of manual labor at first, especially with clearing the land and pre-paring the soil. Once you have the ground ready, seeds take time to germinate, and even then, it may take months before you actually have anything edible coming up from your garden. Disease, pests, poor soil, and even weather will all conspire to keep your garden from producing, so now is the time to perfect your garden, when you don't have to depend on it.

If you live in a condo, townhouse, or apartment, consider practicing your garden-growing skills at a local community garden. This is an especially good choice for those that one day plan to buy a house with some land for that very purpose. Of course, if you plan to indefinitely use your local community garden for your food needs, then you and your neighbors will have to come up with a contingency plan in the event that calamity strikes. Would fellow-community-garden growers be willing to take up arms to protect each other's valuable produce? How will you ensure that the garden stays safe? If you believe that you will end up being a lone wolf, then you might use your community garden as a stepping stone to your future homesteading plans, and really secure your city dwelling for container gardening. Container gardens are a great alternative for spaces where traditional gardening is either not possible, i.e., balconies, decks, and patios, or an area where the soil is not nutritious enough for a proper ground-based garden. People who want to green up their rental apartments, senior citizens who are limited in physical mobility, or those who lack the time to care for a tradition garden will find container gardening perfectly suited to their needs. Absolute beginners will find container gardening easy and rewarding as they develop the skills they need for more complex gardening.

A common outgrowth of gardening is canning. If we do go through a horrible grid-down scenario, there will likely be no power, which in turn means no refrigeration and no ability to freeze your food. Canning will be the simplest way to preserve your fruit and vegetable harvest. I think it's better to purchase and practice with your equipment now, rather than wait until the moment really counts. Consider taking a local gardening class and canning class or take an online gardening class and canning class. Invest in some easy-to-follow gardening books and canning books, as there are numerous ones to choose from.

So what should my plan be?

Here is my recommendation, kind of a recap of my food summary, and I am happy for someone to tell me otherwise, but I think if you are looking to build up your food storage, it should go something like this.

1. Start planning a garden now. Next year's growing season will be here sooner than you think. Now is the time to get your property cleared and the soil ready to grow your fruits and vegetables.

Read books on gardening and canning, as well as take classes for both. Even if your garden isn't producing anything yet, go to your local farmer's market and buy produce to practice canning with.

2. Build up the stores of food that you normally eat, until you have at least 6 months' worth. This is a shorter-term goal, should there be a shorter-term recovery after a catastrophe.

3. Once you have 6 months' worth of food, you should look into long-term storable food. This is food that will last you for years, even decades. These are the type of foods that don't need to be rotated and will give you a great option for supplementing your regular meals, if needed.

4. Use and rotate your food stores. This will accomplish two things. First, it will give you exposure to the menu options you have, and secondly, it will allow you to keep your inventory fresh.

Are there other food options? Yes, there are so many different ways to provide food for your family, from sprouting to livestock, but what has been discussed in this chapter up to this point is an easy path for the beginner to take. It's better to start small and work up to bigger and better food options than to become overwhelmed and throw your hands up, without doing anything at all: worst case scenario—you will at least have something to eat.

Eat-On-The-Go

Your food-on-the-go should consist of packaged meals that are ready to eat or easy to prepare, so that you can save time and fuel resources. Leave your organic, vegan, health-food-store diet for times of peace, but for bugging out, think war rations. (Maybe an entrepreneuring health-food specialist will come up with something that will fit the bill for both.)

In this instance, I promote food that meets the following criteria:

- long shelf life
- lightweight
- high in carbs and calories
- won't leak or crush easily

My everyday diet is protein rich, but bugging out is not my day job, only my weekend-warrior playtime. Carbohydrates are converted into sugars, which our bodies burn as energy. This "fuel" is critical in keeping us mentally and physically energized. So, forget the Atkins diet, chow down on complex carbohydrates.

Meals Ready to Eat (MRE)

Our soldiers are issued MREs while serving in the field. Essentially, these are completely self-contained meal kits. They typically contain an entrée, a side dish, large cracker, small dessert, condiment pack, and a flameless ration heater. A flameless ration heater, or FRH, is a water-activated, exothermic-chemical heater. The ration heater contains finely powdered magnesium metal, alloyed with a small amount of iron, and table salt. To activate the reaction, a small amount of water is added, and the boiling point of water is quickly reached as the reaction proceeds.

These meal kits are time-tested in war, are somewhat nutritious, and have high-calorie content—typically 1200+ per meal. The government restricts the sale of official MREs, but you can easily find them on *eBay*, *Craigslist*, at Army/Navy surplus stores, and at gun shows.

MREs tend to be of on the heavy side, but consider the fact that you don't have to add water to reconstitute them, as you would dehydrated or freeze-dried food. This is a big plus because you only need a couple of tablespoons of water to activate the flameless ration heater. This will save you from a lot of water weight (no pun intended). If you want to lighten your load even more, consider "field stripping" your MREs by removing everything but the main entrée, which of course is going to be the most filling and give you the most calories for the size. I tell people that MREs are like flattened, canned food that lasts almost 10yrs (when not exposed to excessive heat).

First Strike Ration (FSR)

The development of the FSR came from the fact that prior to deployment, soldiers would "field strip" their MREs. Field stripping an MRE involves removing all the excess MRE packaging and unwanted items, i.e., bags, boxes, heaters, extra spoons, accessory packs, etc. Creative field stripping could reduce 3 MREs (one day's worth) down to the same size as a single MRE. While this practice reduced the soldier's load by only packing the most critical MRE parts, it also led to increased waste and a reduced consumption of food. A single FSR, which is 24-hours' worth of food, is approximately 50% the size and weight of three MREs. They are harder to find than MREs but are always available on eBay.

1 FSR = 2,900 calories

3 MREs = 3,800 calories

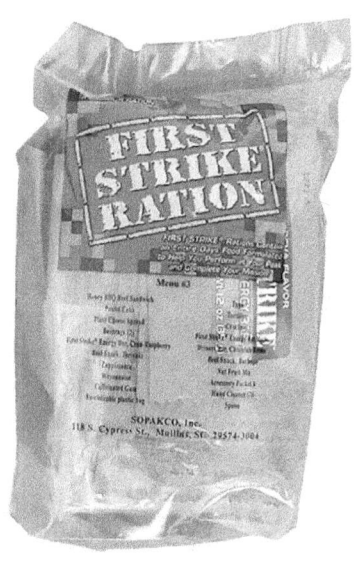

My everyday carry and get-home bag roll with FSRs. I abide by the military acronym of KISS: Keep it simple stupid. In this way, I have three compact meals that don't need water, that have a super-long shelf life, that have their own heat source or can be eaten cold, along with being wrapped in water-proof packaging. They can practically be run over by a truck and still be ready for battle—these are the Cadillacs of food rations for urban go bags.

Freeze-Dried Pouches
Most, if not all, outdoor retailers sell freeze-dried camping meals designed for backpacking enthusiasts. I've seen them at Wal-Mart, but Amazon.com has more variety. They come as an entrée, are surprisingly tasty, and are an excellent, light-weight, BOB meal option, and have an even longer shelf-life than an MRE.

Because these meal options are freeze-dried, they need to be reconstituted with water. You will need a heat source, such as a camp fire or an ultra-light camp stove, to prepare these meals. Depending on the circumstances, bringing water to a boil is not always the safest, most convenient option, as an open flame, combined with the aroma of a tasty, hot meal might draw a hungry mob. I constantly hear people say how lightweight they are; well, of course they are since they don't have any water weight. When comparing MREs/FSRs to freeze-dried pouches, we are comparing apples and oranges. The point is, don't forget to carry extra water, otherwise, your food will be hydrated, leaving you dehydrated instead.

Bars

Energy bars, protein bars, candy bars, and granola bars are the most practical eat-on-the-go mini-meals available. There are hundreds of different brands and varieties to choose from. A fistful of these could keep you bugging out for days. They would not be a long-term solution, but perfect for very short-term use. Some of their many advantages include being:

- packed with carbohydrates
- oftentimes high-calorie
- compact and light-weight
- affordable
- sold everywhere
- of a huge variety
- prepackaged in single servings

Do your research by comparing brands and types of bars for such things as:

- price
- quality
- carbs
- protein
- fat
- calories
- sugar content
- gluten-free (if required)
- non-GMO (preferable)
- organic (preferable)

Homemade MREs

You can actually assemble your own MRE. Your grocery store will have all of the ingredients that you will need. Your personalized MRE will not have the long shelf life that the military MRE will, but at least you can customize it to your liking. Making your own MREs will also be less expensive than purchasing traditional ones. When determining what kind of food items to include, make sure that they do not require refrigeration, that they require little to no cooking, and if necessary, only water for reconstitution. Here is a list of foods that you can consider:

- Tasty Bite makes Indian and Asian food pouches that are all natural, vegetarian, gluten-free, MSG-free, preservative-free, kosher, and fully cooked.
- Knorr Pasta Sides
- Bear Creek Soup Mix
- Uncle Ben's Ready Rice pouches (comes in many types and flavors)
- Idahoan Loaded Baked Mashed Potatoes
- Ova Easy Egg Crystals
- Honey Stinger Organic Waffles
- Honey sticks

- Packaged snack crackers and cheese spread
- Pouches of tuna
- Tanka Bar Natural Buffalo Bars
- Beef/turkey jerky
- Peanut butter/apple sauce squeeze packs
- Mini candy bars
- GU Energy Gel
- Instant drink mixes, i.e., coffee, tea, Carnation Instant Breakfast, Gatorade, hot cocoa, etc.
- Granola/cereal bars
- Instant oatmeal
- Maruchan Ramen Noodle Soup (can be eaten uncooked, if necessary)
- GORP ("good ole' raisins and peanuts" or do a Google search for an endless amount of GORP, trail-mix recipes with ingredients such as dried fruits, roasted nuts, various cereals, dried hot peppers, chocolate-covered coffee beans, etc.)
- Gum
- Multi-vitamins/multi-minerals/ Emergen-C
- Single servings of salt, pepper, hot sauce, non-dairy creamer, sugar, ketchup, etc.
- Bouillon cubes
- Spork or plastic utensils
- Moist wipes/paper napkins
- Toilet paper
- Matches
- Baby-food pouches
- Infant formula, single-serve packet

Dig through your stockpile and arrange the types of meals/snacks/drinks/deserts you want to package together. Remember to diversify your "MREs" if you don't want the same, boring meal every time you tear into one. This is especially important for children and the elderly, who are susceptible to food fatigue.

In order to create your own "MRE," use a vacuum sealer to package an array of food items of your liking. Vacuum sealing the meals not only helps to preserve them longer but also waterproofs them. The added bonus is that they are also organized and very compact, which are two essential qualities to a well-packed bug-out bag!

Ensure that you label the contents, along with the packing date, with a permanent marker. It would also be proactive to list the best by date next to the content names listed, although the food items should still be edible past this date due to the vacuum sealing.

6
HEATING AND COOKING

Staying Warm Without a Heating Source

Clothing

Layering your clothing is a tried-and-true way to maximize your comfort indoors and outdoors. The beauty of this simple concept is that it allows you to make quick adjustments based on your activity level and changes in the weather. Each layer has a function. The base layer (against your skin) manages moisture; the mid layer is designed to offer a slight boost in warmth without adding a lot of extra bulk; the insulating layer protects you from the cold; and the shell layer (outer layer) shields you from wind and rain. You simply add or subtract layers as needed. As a rule of thumb, you should expect to be a little chilly when you first start out the day and when you take a break from an activity. After a few minutes of steady movement, your body will start to produce more heat. If you're wearing too many layers to start with, you'll most likely get too hot after about 15-20 minutes of activity. When in doubt, wear your warmest layer when you start your activity, but remove it at the first sign of overheating or perspiration. Also, don't forget your extremities. Unless it's the middle of summer and you're close to the equator, always pack a warm hat and gloves, just in case the weather turns ugly. If you buy a new jacket and it fits perfectly with just a

T-shirt, you may want to get the next size up so you'll have room to layer additional clothing underneath.

Move to One Room
Instead of trying to heat the whole house, focus your attention on heating just one room instead. One way to do this is to use a main room of the house for the family's activities/sleeping quarters; essentially, the body heat of each family member will create a "group heater" so to speak. Try to pick a room that gets a lot of natural sunlight and already has a heating source, such as a fireplace or pot belly stove. Ideally, you would pick a windowed room on the southwest side of your home. The collective body heat from your family, along with the heat generated from your single-room heating source will keep everyone nice and toasty.

"We're Not Heating the Neighborhood!"

You probably remember being a child and hearing your parents yell out the words, "We're not trying to heat the neighborhood!" Yes, there are the obvious ways of preventing this from happening, like shutting the doors of the house that lead to the outside or closing the windows when you want to trap the heat in, but there are other sneaky ways that heat can dissipate from the house that need to be guarded against.

Close off any unused rooms. The closed door makes that room another barrier between you and the frigid outdoors. It also stops air from circulating as much, which reduces heat loss. Keep your windows air-tight. You may want to purchase removable window-caulk or plastic to better seal them. At a minimum, stuff a towel or shirt in front of any noticeable leaks. Seal your doors. Check around the door frame and also under the door. You may want to buy weather stripping or a door sweep. Again, at minimum, make a draft dodger or stuff a towel at the bottom of the door. Add insulation in the attic and the crawl space. A lot of heat escapes through the attic, as warm air rises and cold air sinks. Make sure that your attic has enough insulation.

Drapes and Shower Curtains over Windows

Drapes (the thicker the better) are one of the main ways to protect your house from losing heat through the windows. Of course, open them when the sun is shining and close them when it's not. Closing your drapes as soon as dusk falls will maximize your house's potential to retain that heat.

Another way to improve upon your windows is to cover them with shower curtains. Remove the shower curtain from the bathroom (without power no one is going to want to take a cold shower anyway) and drape across the window, then carefully tape or attach the clear shower curtain to the wall so that natural light can come through the window/curtain while preventing hot air from leaving through the window. You might want to purchase extras, as you may not have enough shower curtains to cover the most important, light-bearing windows of the house. This will keep the cold air out and the warmth from the sun in.

Rugs or Carpet
Make sure that heat isn't escaping through the floor either. Take rugs and mats from around the home and lay them down in your room. They will add a few layers between you and the cold floor.

Tents in the Living Room

Another great idea is to set up tents inside your living room. One family had a tent for the boys and a tent for the girls. This trapped in the heat to an even more confined area inside their living room.

Leave During the Day

Make the family go outside and soak up the rays during the day. Obviously, if there is a winter storm, you'll have to stay indoors, otherwise make your home a warm location to return to at the end of the day instead of a frigid jail.

Eat Before You Go To Bed

By eating before you go to bed, your body will be digesting during the night time—keeping you a little warmer than normal as you sleep.

Drink Warm Beverages

Warm beverages will raise your core body temperature. The process can be very relaxing and even stimulating, too. Make a cup of hot cocoa, tea, coffee, or sip on some warm broth.

Let as much sun hit your house as possible.

Check for obstructions, i.e., plants, sheds, etc., that might keep the sun's rays from reaching your house. Remove items leaning against walls on the sunny side of your house. (Ideally, put them back again at night for additional insulation).

Candles

Candles can produce a lot of heat, but just be mindful of where they are placed and do not leave them unattended. A trip to most any grocery store or discount store can provide you with a number of candles for a very inexpensive price!

Exercise

Exercising vigorously for 20 minutes can warm you up and keep you warm well after the exercise session. Plus, a healthy body is generally more tolerant of the cold.

Be Active

Moving around produces body heat! The more active you are, the better your blood circulation will be. This means that warm blood gets to your fingers and toes, keeping them warm.

Snuggle

The living body of any warm-blooded animal is a furnace unto itself. Snuggle with your cat or dog to keep each other warm. Better yet, snuggle with you sweetheart, but read the warning below before going any further.

Warning

This may be well known, but not thought of often, so be reminded that it is a common phenomenon that there is a spike in births nine months after blackouts, power outages, etc., so have your double-barrier method in place, just as all of your other preps are, if you know what I mean.

Heating Options

Coal stores well if kept in a dark place and away from moving air. Air speeds deterioration and breakdown, causing it to burn more rapidly. Coal may be stored in a plastic-lined pit or in sheds, bags, boxes, or barrels, and should be kept away from circulating air, light, and moisture. Cover it to lend protection from weather and sun.

Hardwoods such as apple, cherry, and other fruit woods are slow burning and sustain coals. Hardwoods are more difficult to burn than softer woods, thus requiring a supply of kindling. Soft woods such as pine and cedar are light in weight and burn very rapidly, leaving ash and few coals for cooking. Firewood is usually sold by the cord, which is a neat pile that totals 128 cubic ft. This pile is 4 ft. wide, 4 ft. high, and 8 ft. long. Some dealers sell wood by the ton. As a general rule of thumb, a standard cord of air-dried, dense hardwood weighs about 2 tons and provides as much heat as 1 ton of coal. Be suspicious of any alleged cord delivered in a 1/2 or 3/4 ton pickup truck.

If you use your firewood throughout the entire day for five months during the winter season, it's likely you will need 1 ½ cords. If you only use your firewood in the evenings during that 5-month span, a cord will be sufficient. If you only use your fireplace or wood/coal burning stove a few days during the week, a ½ cord should be enough. These are just estimates, as you may have multiple fire places or want to store more for barter purposes.

For best results, wood should be seasoned (dried) properly for at least a year. You need to rely on visual clues to determine if your firewood is suitable for burning. Seasoned wood will have checked or cracked ends. Often times the bark will separate easily from the wood. It may have a grey, weathered appearance, but not if it has been stored under cover. If you knock two pieces together it should sound hollow, instead of dense.

A plastic tarp, wood planks, or other plastic or metal sheeting over the woodpile is useful in keeping the wood dry, as well as storing it in full sun. This method stops bugs and bark beetles from living in and off your wood. Improperly stored wood can result in unwanted moisture and rot. Wood is best stored about 10 ft. from your house to minimize pests and insects in your home. Firewood should be stored at least 6 in. from the ground, with the bark side facing up to help shed rain. A 2-3 day supply of firewood should be kept inside your house. Wood that is brought in from outside is often too cold to result in proper combustion when starting a fire and will cool down your fire too much. Other types of fuels are more practical to store and use than wood or coal.

Newspaper logs make a good and inexpensive source of fuel. You may prepare the logs in the following manner: use about 8 pages of newspaper and open flat. Spread the stack, alternating the cut sides and folded sides. Place a 1-in. wood dowel or metal rod across one end and roll the paper around the rod very tightly. Roll it up until there is 6-8 in. left to roll, and then slip another 8 pages underneath the roll. Continue this procedure until you have a roll 4-6 in. in diameter. With a fine wire, tie the roll on both ends. Withdraw the rod. Your newspaper log is ready to use. Four of these logs will burn about 1 hour.

Propane is another excellent fuel for indoor use. Like kerosene, it produces carbon dioxide as it burns and therefore is not poisonous. It does consume oxygen so be sure to crack a window when burning propane. Propane stores indefinitely, having no known shelf life. Propane stoves and small portable heaters are very economical, simple to use, and come the closest to approximating the type of convenience most of us are accustomed to using on a daily basis. The storage of propane is governed by strict local laws. Please check the laws governing propane in your city or county. The primary hazard in using propane is that it is heavier than air and if a leak occurs it may "pool," which can create an explosive atmosphere. Furthermore, basement, natural-gas heating units CANNOT be legally converted for propane use. Again, the vapors are heavier than air and form "pockets." Ignition sources such as water heaters and electrical sources can cause an explosion.

White Gas (Coleman fuel) is another fuel option. Many families have camp stoves which burn Coleman fuel or white gasoline. These stoves are fairly easy to use and produce a great amount of heat. However, they, like charcoal, produce vast amounts of carbon monoxide.

NEVER use a Coleman Fuel stove indoors. It could be a fatal mistake to your entire family. Never store fuels in the house or near a heater.

Use a metal storage cabinet which can be locked and is vented on the top and on the bottom.

Kerosene (Range Oil No. 1) is the cheapest of all the storage fuels and is also very forgiving if you make a mistake. Kerosene is not as explosive as gasoline and Coleman fuel. Kerosene stores well for long periods of time, and by introducing some fuel additives, it can be made to store even longer. However, do not store it in metal containers for extended periods of time, unless they are porcelain lined, because the moisture in the kerosene will rust through the container, causing the kerosene to leak out. Most hardware stores and home-improvement centers sell kerosene in 5-gal., plastic containers. A 55-gal. drum store in the back yard, or 10 plastic containers, 5 gal. each, will provide fuel enough to last an entire winter if used sparingly. These containers can be stored for many years.

Caution: To burn kerosene you will need a kerosene heater. There are many models and sizes to choose from, but remember that you are not trying to heat your entire home. The larger the heater, the more fuel you will have to store. Most families should be able to get by on a heater that produces about 9,600 BTUs of heat, though kerosene heaters are made that will produce up to 25,000 to 30,000 BTUs. If you have the storage space to store the fuel required by these larger heaters, they are excellent investments, but for most families the smaller heaters are more than adequate. When selecting a kerosene heater, be sure to get one that can double as a cooking surface and source of light. Then when you are forced to use it, be sure to plan your meals so that they can be cooked when you are using the heater for heat rather than wasting fuel used for cooking only. When kerosene burns, it requires very little oxygen as compared to charcoal. You must crack a window open to allow enough oxygen to enter the room to prevent asphyxiation.

During combustion, kerosene is not poisonous and is safe to use indoors. To prevent possible fires you should always fill it outside, though.

The momentary, incomplete combustion during lighting and extinguishing of kerosene heaters can cause some unpleasant odors. To prevent these odors from lingering in your home, always light and extinguish the heater out of doors. During normal operation, a kerosene heater is practically odorless.

Charcoal should never be burned indoors. When charcoal burns it is a voracious consumer of oxygen and will quickly deplete the oxygen supply in your little "home within a home." Furthermore, as it burns, it produces vast amounts of carbon monoxide, which is a deadly poison and could prove fatal to your entire family.

Cooking

To conserve your cooking-fuel, always do your emergency cooking in the most efficient manner as possible. Don't boil more water than you need, extinguish the fire as soon as you're finished cooking, and plan your meals ahead of time to con-solidate as much cooking as you can. During the winter, cook on top of your heating unit while heating your home, and cook in a pressure cooker or other fuel-efficient container as often as feasible. Keep enough fuel to provide cooking for at least 7 to 10 days.

It is even possible to cook without using fuel at all. For example, to cook dry beans you can place them inside a pressure cooker with the proper amount of water and other ingredients needed, and place it on your heat source until it comes up to pressure. Then turn off the heat, remove the pressure cooker, and place inside a large box filled with newspapers, blankets, or other insulating materials. Leave it 2 ½ hours and then open it. Your meal will be done, having cooked for 2 ½ hours with no heat.

If you don't have a large box in which to place the pressure cooker, simply wrap it in several blankets and place it in the corner.

Store matches in a waterproof, airtight container with each piece of equipment that must be lit with a flame.

Sterno fuel, a jellied-petroleum product, is an excellent source of fuel for inclusion in your back pack as part of your 72-hour kit. Sterno is very lightweight and easily ignited with a match or a spark from flint and steel, but is not explosive. It is also safe for use indoors. A Sterno stove can be purchased at any sporting-goods store and many drug stores and will retail between $3 and $8, depending upon the model you choose. They fold up into a very small, compact unit, which is ideal for carrying in a pack.

One can (about the diameter of a can of tuna fish and twice as high) will allow you to cook 6 meals if used frugally. Chafing dishes and fondue pots can also be used with Sterno. It is not without some complications: It will evaporate very easily, even when the lid is securely fastened. If you use Sterno in your 72-hour kit, you should check it every 6-8 months to insure that it has not evaporated beyond the point of usage. Because of this issue, it is not a good fuel for long-term storage. It is a costly fuel to use compared to others available, but is extremely convenient and portable.

White gas, or Coleman fuel, when used with a Coleman stove, is another excellent and convenient fuel for cooking. It is not as portable or as lightweight as Sterno, but produces a much greater BTU value. Like Sterno, Coleman fuel has a tendency to evaporate even when the container is tightly sealed, so it is not a good fuel for long-term storage. Unlike Sterno, it is highly volatile and will explode under the right conditions; therefore, it should never be stored in the home. Because of its highly flammable nature, great care should always be exercised when lighting stoves and lanterns that use Coleman fuel.

Many serious burns have been caused by carelessness with this product. Always store Coleman fuel in the garage or shed.

Charcoal is the least expensive fuel per BTU that the average family can store. Remember that it must always be used outside because of the vast amounts of poisonous carbon monoxide it produces.

Charcoal will store for an extended period of time if it's stored in air tight containers. It readily absorbs moisture from the surrounding air, so don't store it in the paper bags it comes in for more than a few months or it may be difficult to light. Transfer it to airtight metal or plastic containers where it will keep almost indefinitely. About $60 worth of charcoal will provide all the cooking fuel a family will need for an entire year if used sparingly. The best time to buy briquettes inexpensively is at the end of the summer. Broken or torn bags of briquettes are usually sold at a big discount.

You will also want to store a small amount of lighter fluid or kerosene. Newspapers will also provide an excellent ignition source for charcoal when used in a funnel type of lighting device. To light charcoal using newspapers, use 2-3 sheets that are crumpled up and a #10 tin can. Cut both ends out of the can. Punch holes every two inches around the lower edge of the can with a punch-type can opener (for opening juice cans). Set the can down so the punches/holes are on the bottom. Place the crumpled newspaper in the bottom of the can and place the charcoal briquettes on top of the newspaper. Lift the can slightly and light the newspaper. Prop a small rock under the bottom edge of the can to create a good draft. The briquettes will be ready to use in about 20-30 minutes.

When the coals are ready, remove the chimney and place them in your cooker. Never place burning charcoal directly on concrete or cement because the heat will crack it. A wheelbarrow or old metal garbage can lid makes an excellent container for this type of fire.

One of the nice things about charcoal is that you can regulate the heat you will receive from them. Each briquette will produce about 40 degrees of heat. If you are baking bread, for example, and need 400 degrees of heat for your oven, simply use ten briquettes.

To conserve heat and thereby get the maximum heat value from your charcoal, you must learn to funnel the heat where you want it rather than letting it dissipate into the air around you. One excellent way to do this is to cook inside a cardboard oven. Take a cardboard box, about the size of an orange crate, and cover it with aluminum foil inside and out. Be sure that the shiny side is visible so that maximum reflectivity is achieved. Turn the box on its side so that the opening is no longer on the top but is on the side. Place some small bricks or other noncombustible material inside, upon which you can rest a cookie sheet (about 2-3 in. above the bottom of the box). Place 10-burning-charcoal briquettes between the bricks (if you need 400 degrees), then the support for your cooking vessels, and lastly, place your bread pans or whatever else you are using on top of the cookie sheet. Prop a foil-covered cardboard lid over the open side, leaving a large crack for air to get in (charcoal needs a lot of air to burn) and bake your bread, cake, cookies, or whatever else, just like you would in your regular oven. You will be amazed by the results!

To make your own charcoal, select twigs, limbs, and branches of fruit, nut, and other hardwood trees; black walnuts, and peach or apricot pits may also be used. Cut wood into the desired size, place in a large can which has a few holes punched into it, put a lid on the can, and place in a hot fire. When the flames from the holes in the can turn yellow-red, remove the can from the fire and allow it to cool. Store the briquettes in a moisture-proof container. Remember to only burn charcoal in a well-ventilated area.

Wood- and coal-burning stoves have a built-in cooking surface. These are excellent to use indoors during the winter because you may already be using it to heat the home. In the summer, however, they are unbearably hot and impractical for indoor use. If you choose to build a campfire outside, be sure to use caution and follow all the rules for safety. Little children, and even many adults, are not aware of the tremendous dangers that open fires may pose.

Kerosene heaters will also double as cooking units. Only purchase a kerosene heater that can be used to cook on as well. Follow the same precautions for cooking, as was discussed under the section on heating with kerosene.

Propane camp stoves are generally a family's first choice. They are the most convenient and easy to use of all emergency-cooking appliances available. They may be used indoors or outdoors. As with any other emergency-fuel source, cook with a pressure cooker whenever possible to conserve fuel.

Solar oven

A lot of urban survivalists (myself included) are planning on using some of the different heating options as mentioned previously. Longer term planning, though, raises the question, "What do I do when those options runs out?" I suggest giving some thought to how you'll prepare food and heat water without any liquid or gas fuel whatsoever.

One option is a solar oven. A solar oven can be as simple as a box lined with aluminum foil, or my preference, the Global Sun Oven. The Global Sun Oven is the world's most widely used solar oven. Solar cooking has been around for centuries, but up until now, not many people have had the opportunity to try cooking with the sun. Using the most advanced materials, the Sun Oven takes all the hassles out of solar cooking to create the ultimate solar appliance. It will reach temperatures of 360-400 degrees Fahrenheit. The sun oven can be used in the winter as well as in the summer. It has been used very successfully at below-zero conditions at a base camp on Mt. Everest. It measures 19" x 19" with an average depth of 11". The total weight is only 21 lbs. It is currently being used in over 126 countries around the world.

If you're like me, anything that is overly complicated or inconvenient is rarely used, and that is why I love the Sun Oven. It's portable enough to be taken on camping trips, light enough for my kids to carry, and the set-up takes less than a minute. As long as there is sunshine, this baby can cook anything from hard-boiled eggs, to roasted chicken, to casseroles, to cookies, to pizza, and more. I saw a *YouTube* video where the person made homemade chicken soup with a simple combination of noodles, veggies, water, and raw chicken...yes, RAW chicken. As the soup heats up and cooks, the chicken and water create a rich broth, so you don't have to use canned broth or bouillon cubes for flavor.

You can even pasteurize water in a solar oven. Water actually pasteurizes at temperatures below boiling, and I discovered a terrific, low-tech method to determine when water is safe to drink. The Water Pasteurization Indicator (WAPI) is a simple, small, polycarbonate tube that contains a small amount of wax. This wax melts at the same temperature required for pasteurization of water and milk. Dangle the WAPI into a container of water, and when the wax is melted, you know the water is safe to drink! When the WAPI is removed from the water, the wax hardens, and it's ready to use again and again... brilliant!

With solar ovens, you never have to worry about fuel, and this is a big advantage. The cooking process may take a bit more time, depending on the type of oven you use and how much sunlight is available at the time, but you can help the oven cook faster by refocusing it toward the sun every half hour or so. This is just a simple process of angling the oven in the direction of the sun, taking no more than a minute or so.

On overcast days, a solar oven isn't going to work, but there are other options for grid-free and fuel-free cooking. Take a look at stoves that require very small amounts of charcoal or wood. Although wood is technically a fuel, it isn't something you normally have to purchase, as it is readily available in nature. The StoveTec rocket stove is an example of this type of stove. It's small and portable, and as long as you know how to start a compact fire by using tinder and small sticks, you're good to go. Along with a stove of this type, you'll need a few pieces of cookware that can be used over an open flame, and then plenty of practice!

In summary, each cooking method has its own pros and cons, but the only way to know which one will work best for you is to experiment with these varied options.

Cast Iron Cookware

In a long-term crisis, daily life will move to a much more basic level similar to the "olden days" or life in third-world countries. When this happens, nothing will beat cooking with cast iron. Settlers and cattle drivers used it for many reasons, and there are many reasons why YOU should use it too.

Cost Effective
Compared to hoity-toity cookware sold in many stores, cast-iron is cheap! It's plentiful as well. You can find cast-iron cookware at many lawn sales and most flea markets for just a few bucks. Because it distributes and holds heat so well, it also requires a tad-less fuel. What's more, it lasts forever.

Rugged
These pots and pans won't scratch, chip, or melt. They'll withstand extremely high temperatures, and you can clock somebody with a cast-iron skillet if you run out of ammo. The fact that it distributes heat so well makes it particularly useful for inconsistent flames—like campfires!

Versatile
You can use your cast iron skillet on the kitchen stove, in the oven, or directly on campfire coals. You can use it for pan frying, deep frying, roasting, and stewing. A basic skillet and Dutch oven will cover most cooking needs.

Taste
Food cooked in cast iron tastes better in many cases.

Health Benefits
Did you know that the non-stick Teflon coating they put on pans (the stuff that always peels off unless you cook with plastic spatulas and such) will actually KILL pet birds? These chemicals get released in the air when you heat it up. These pans often come with attached warnings. You're eating that when you cook with it. Cast iron is often associated with high-fat foods like rich deserts and bacon, but that's just because of its "old time" reputation. A properly seasoned, older skillet actually requires LESS oil to cook with than a traditional pan. Also, cooking with cast iron boosts

your iron intake, because trace amounts of it gets absorbed by the food. This "iron benefit" will be particularly beneficial in a survival situation. In fact, cooking foods in cast iron can double or triple the iron content of a meal. People at risk of iron deficiency are pregnant women, infants and toddlers, teenage girls, and anyone that has suffered blood loss.

Are there disadvantages to cast iron?
It's heavy. If it's not properly cared for it may rust. It's not dishwasher safe (a moot point in a post-grid scenario). Foods which are very acidic (i.e., beans, tomatoes, citrus juices, etc.) should not be cooked in seasoned cast iron until the cookware is highly seasoned. The high acidity of these foods will strip the seasoning and result in discoloration and metallic tasting food. Enameled cast iron is not affected by acidity and can be used with all foods, but cannot be used over campfires or open grills, so it is best to just stick to your well-seasoned cast iron for its cooking versatility.

Seasoning, Care, and Use
New cast-iron cookware has a grey tint to it, but a well-seasoned piece is black. You can buy new pieces already seasoned, but if you want to (or need to) season it on your own, heat your oven to 300 degrees, coat the unit in vegetable shortening, lard, or vegetable oil, then put it in the oven, remove after 15 minutes to pour out excess grease, and bake for an hour. If food sticks to the surface or you notice a dull, grey color, repeat the seasoning process. It usually will take about four sessions of doing this for the seasoning to totally take hold. I personally use vegetable oil (any high-smoke-point cooking oil should work, i.e., sunflower, safflower, coconut, peanut, grapeseed,

sesame, etc.) for health and religious reasons, since we do not use lard in our household. We don't use vegetable shortening in our house either due to trans-fatty acids. The more often your cast iron goes through this process, the better it will become. Seasoning (and general use) fills pores in the iron resulting in a protective, non-stick coating (eventually).

To clean your cast iron, wash by hand only, using mild, soapy water. Once washed, dry immed-iately—even before first use. Don't use strong detergents or metal scouring pads, as they remove seasoning. However, consider that cookware gets to 400 ^{o} F in 4 minutes on medium heat and is sterile at 212° F, so soap isn't always necessary. Store the pans in a dry location, with the cover off, so moisture doesn't build up.

Rub with a light coat of vegetable oil after every wash. Use enough to restore the sheen, but without making it sticky.

This will keep your cast iron seasoned and protect it from moisture.

Because you create, maintain, and even repair the seasoning, your cookware can last for 100 years or more.

Use metal, wood, or hi-temperature silicone utensils. The handles get very hot, so use mitts when touching the handles and use trivets to protect countertops from hot cookware.

Cast iron rarely needs to go above a medium heat setting when properly pre-heated. For the times when you do cook at higher temperatures, add oil to cookware just before adding food to prevent sticking. Some foods may stick to new cookware (especially eggs). Use a little extra oil or butter until you've built up the seasoning. When deep frying, fill cookware only to 1/3 of its capacity. Gas flames should not extend up the sides of cookware.

Match pan size to burner size.

Cast iron is right at home on induction, ceramic, electric, and gas cooktops, in your oven, on the grill, or even over the campfire. On glass or ceramic cooktops, lift cookware, never slide it.

Do not use in the microwave. (In a disaster scenario, the microwave will be out-of-commission, plus, it isn't the healthiest cooking method anyway). What's nice about cast iron is that it is perfect for use now and in a post-apocalyptic scenario. This will save you money in the long run, rather than buying separate cookware for then and now.

Don't panic if your iron cookware accidentally becomes rusty. It's really easy to fix. Scour the rust, rinse, dry, and rub with a little vegetable oil.

If the problem persists, you will need to thoroughly remove all rust and follow the re-seasoning instructions as listed above.

Cast-iron-skillet trivia
Lewis and Clark listed their Dutch oven as one of their most critical pieces of equipment.

George Washington's mother thought so highly of her cast iron that she put it in her will.

Carbon Steel

Do you love cast iron but hate the weight? Well, there is another option that may tickle your fancy. Have you ever thought of investing in carbon steel instead? Carbon steel is similar to cast iron in durability and conductivity, but thinner and about half the weight. It heats and cools fast (although not nearly that of copper or even aluminum), making it ideal for on-the-go use. Yes, it's certainly much healthier to use carbon steel vs. aluminum and Teflon, but it isn't going to impart iron into the food like cast iron will.

It's actually less brittle than its counterpart, so there's less risk of it breaking when dropped or smashed. Be careful when purchasing carbon steel, though—too thin and you can find yourself with a warped skillet—a common complaint from users of cheaper carbon steel. Carbon steel doesn't retain heat quite as well, but most people say they don't notice a significant difference. Some users say that they find hot spots in their carbon-steel frying pans, but this can be avoided by buying them a little thicker and from a reputable seller.

Carbon-steel skillets have smaller pores, making for a very smooth surface, allowing for easier seasoning. Just one application of oil should be enough to make them nonstick. Newer, cast-cooking vessels, however, hold their seasonings better because of their rougher texture, due to deeper pores on the metal's surface. This may not be the case if you are looking at U.S., pre-WWII, cast-iron examples, which were ground smoother and a bit thinner. Carbon steel will still require maintenance to make it last (several lifetimes if used and not abused).

Cast iron may survive a bout with acidic foods or even submersion into soapy water; the same doesn't go for carbon steel, however. Both of those instances would strip the seasoning right off of carbon-steel cookware.

Ultimately, cast iron and carbon steel are very similar products. It all boils down to personal preference—and what's in your wallet, I suppose. Just remember that carbon steel tends to run about double the price as compared to their cast-iron counterparts.

7
PERSONAL HYGIENE

Staying clean by today's standards will be next to impossible in a post-apocalyptic world. The daily, sometimes twice daily, bath or shower will become a rarity (unless you consider bathing in the river/lake during favorable weather is a bath). The world will be vastly different, but the same germs will still be just as prevalent, if not more so, since stringent hygiene and cleaning will be a thing of the past. The only advantage that you will have then, that most do not have now, is the fact that contact with other people will be limited to you and the people trying to survive alongside of you (assuming that you haven't ended up in a FEMA camp). Taking some basic steps in personal hygiene will be a huge benefit to everyone in the group by not only helping to prevent disease, but by also contributing to your comfort.

The no brainer here is the continuation of proper hand washing or use of hand sanitizer. Since the average person touches their face more than 2,000 times per day and the mouth, eyes, and nose are the most likely portals of entry for germs, this will be imperative in preventing infections. This is especially important to consider when preparing food for yourself and others. Hand sanitizer, rubbing alcohol, vinegar, disinfectant wipes, and bleach will all work to clean or sanitize your hands (just make sure that you don't put bleach or alcohol directly on your hands without being diluted). Soap and water is probably the easiest and most common mechanism for keeping the hands clean. Even washing your hands with clean water alone (if you have run out of soap) is better than not washing your hands at all.

Now, for the rest of your body, try other methods for keeping fresh: let your body air out. Even if you are sedentary, your undergarments are going to be packing a pretty powerful punch. Wearing dirty, sweat-soaked clothes, that are in constant contact with your skin, gives bacteria the perfect environment for breeding. At every available opportunity, get as naked as possible and stand in the sun. Better yet, do a little sunbathing. Make sure both your front side and backside take turns. Of course, you don't want to get sunburned, so use your judgment. You may want to use the recommendations given for proper vitamin D absorption from the sun, which will depend on how much skin is exposed and the time of day. Remember that vitamin D will also help to bolster your immune system, which is especially important during a time of emotional and physical stress. If you're fair skinned and sunning yourself outside at noon, you only need a few minutes without sunscreen. If you're already tan or of Hispanic origin, you need maybe 15 to 20 minutes of direct sunlight. Black skin may require six times the sun exposure to make the same vitamin D levels as a very fair-skinned person.

If it's that time of year when mosquitoes, ticks, and other insects abound, then it would be wise to use a natural insect repellant to ward off the bugs or wear loose-fitting, thin, white shorts and t-shirt in order to air out and get a little dose of sun. While you sport your birthday suit, have your spouse or familiar other do a backside check for bites, boils, and insects that may have attached themselves to your nether region. The time for modesty will have long passed by this point.

When you are airing yourself out, take the time to take a splash bath. Clean your feet, crotch, underarms, and face with soap and water or disinfectant/baby wipes. Taking the time to do this will remove a significant amount of germs, prevent chaffing, and will make you feel better overall. You can use corn starch (stock up on organic, as corn is heavily GMO) to powder yourself in your sweatiest areas in order to keep you dry and less smelly. I would stay away from talc powders as there is some concern that talc is carcinogenic.

While we are on the subject of rank clothes, you will need to develop a plan for washing your clothes, which will more than likely need to be done by hand. If possible, you will want to have a "fresh" set of clothes on hand when you do finally find the chance to get a real bath or shower. I do not know of anything much worse than finally getting clean, only to be punished again by being forced to put dirty clothes right back on. You can easily go a week or longer without washing your outer garments, but your undergarments and socks will not last as long. Have extra socks, underwear (or opt out of underwear), and t-shirts available, if possible.

Grooming will help with cleanliness as well. Keeping finger nails and toe nails neat, clean, and trimmed to proper lengths will keep germs from hiding under them. If you happen to be a nail biter, you might want to consider breaking that habit now for obvious reasons. If you have not considered nail clippers/files, scissors, razors, and combs for your bug-out bag, now would be the time to do so.

You will want to keep head and facial hair trimmed as short as possible and run a comb through both daily. Believe it or not, your hair will get so dirty that it will actually cause your scalp to hurt. This will be aggravated by leaving a ponytail in for too long (for our female audience). Avoid scratching your scalp and let the comb do the work when possible. Use dry shampoo as often as needed, especially when your hair is practically dripping with oil. You can use corn starch alone, or mix with equal parts of baking soda to help neutralize odors. Use a shaker to spread throughout the hair, especially near the roots and in the bangs, then "wash out" with your brush.

Treat every scrape, bump, bite, boil, cut, burn, and hangnail as a life-threatening condition. Sanitize the area as soon as time allows with soap and water or another disinfectant, apply an antibiotic ointment, and cover the area with a bandage. If possible, avoid tasks which will unnecessarily introduce germs into the affected area, and avoid food preparation for the group if the troublesome spot is on your hands. Allow the area to get air when you are resting. If the affected area begins to swell, change color, or worsen, you will need to take additional first-aid or medical measures.

Brush and floss your teeth at least once daily, twice if your supplies will allow it. Use a good quality toothpaste, or baking soda, to brush your teeth and make certain to rinse your mouth thoroughly with clean water. If you find yourself without toothpaste, you can still use your tooth-brush to break the buildup loose and rinse your mouth. Some brushing is better than not at all.

172

Due to questions posed regarding the safety of alcohol-based mouthwash, in regard to possibly causing mouth and throat cancer, I am not an advocate of this type of mouthwash. I don't recommend using a hydrogen-peroxide mouthwash either, as there is concern that it can essentially eat through your teeth. You can easily make a safe mouthwash by boiling your favorite herbs in water for 20 minutes, pouring into a bottle, steeping overnight, and straining. (For a more concentrated mouthwash, you may want to steep for a week, while shaking well once daily). Even without mouthwash, gargling vigorously with clean water or a salt-water mix will help keep your mouth clean.

Attempt to take a bath or shower once per week, if time and your water stockpiles allow for it. Over the course of a week you will build up a lot of grime all over your body, especially during the warmer months. A bath will become a real treat and something that you will look forward to. Wash with unscented soap (if allergies are a problem) from head to toe and make certain to scrub the dirty areas very well. Of course, if it comes down to a choice between having clean drinking water and taking a bath, opt for the clean drinking water.

Hygiene Kit

- Unscented soap (for those with allergies)
- Travel shampoo
- Travel bottle of mouthwash
- Hand sanitizer
- Toothpaste
- Dental floss
- Toothbrush
- Q-tips

- Tweezers
- Triple antibiotic ointment
- Baby wipes
- Band-Aids
- Shaving razor
- Small scissors
- Nail clippers with file
- Emory boards
- Hair comb and brush
- Large MicroNet pack towel
- MicroNet pack wash cloth
- Needles
- Corn starch
- Baking soda
- Salt
- Travel washboard
- Laundry detergent
- Toilet paper
- Sunscreen
- Bug repellant
- Absorbine Jr.
- Travel mirror
- Rubbing alcohol
- Hydrogen peroxide

Herbs for Hygiene

Let's take another look at the three most basic components of personal hygiene: cleanliness of body, cleanliness of mouth and prevention of body odor); but this time, let's discover some unorthodox, personal-hygiene methods.

Three easy to grow, perennial herbs that fit these functions perfectly are soapwort, licorice, and sage. Being able to use these three herbs in a pinch can be handy, or they can supplement an existing daily routine as a more natural solution.

Soapwort- (Saponaria officinalis)

Soap Substitute

Soapwort is a beautiful perennial plant that is hardy in US zones 3-9. It grows to be about 3-ft tall and prefers rich, compost-heavy soil. It can be a little finicky about light requirements, as it likes sun, but not too much afternoon sun. If it likes its growing location, it can become invasive, but if that happens, just harvest more of it. Soapwort leaves and roots can be dried in order to preserve it for later use. (It will still create a lather in this state.)

To make a soapwort-soap solution, use 1 tbsp. of dried leaves or roots (3 tbsp. if the herb is fresh) per 1 cup of water. Bring the water to a boil, add the herb, allow to simmer for 10-15 min, then strain and cool before use.

Soapwort solution can be used for hair, skin, and clothing. It is very gentle and is often found in high-end, organic, facial-care products. It can also be used to clean antique textiles. With all of these uses, why not start using this concoction now?

Soapwort is toxic to fish, so don't wash with or dump soapwort solution directly into a pond or stream where fish are present.

Licorice Root- (Glycyrrhiza glabra)

Toothbrush/Toothpaste Substitute

Another perennial used for cleanliness is the 3-4 ft. licorice plant. Licorice is hardy in USDA gardening zones 7-9. It prefers full sun and moist soil, but doesn't appreciate clay.

The plant will need to grow for 2-3 years before the roots are large enough to harvest. Once they have matured, they should be harvested in the fall, when the plant has focused all of its resources down into the roots before winter. The flavor and chemistry of the roots will be at their peak during this time.

Not only does licorice root contain antibacterial and anti-inflammatory components, it's also shaped perfectly for turning into a simple toothbrush substitute. You can use the licorice root in addition to a regular toothbrush/toothpaste routine, but some people successfully use licorice root alone.

Licorice root typically grows in a long, thin shape. Once it has been dried (this technique won't work on a fresh root), choose one end of the root and soften it by standing it in a glass filled with ½ in. of water or by sucking on it until the root softens (usually about 60 seconds either way). Peel back the outer root bark (the brown looking skin on the root) and gently chew the root until there is a quarter inch or so of "brush" at the end. Gently rub along the gum line and over each tooth to clean the mouth.

Licorice has a sweet taste, so no need to worry about an unusual flavor. After each use, trim away the used "brush" with a knife or scissors and store in a clean place until next use.

As was discussed, it will take a lengthy amount of time to establish this plant in order to really use it for this purpose, so start a licorice garden now.

Sage- (Salvia officinalis)

Deodorant substitute

Sage is a small to medium perennial herb that prefers a very sunny location with dry, well-drained soil. It will grow from zones 4-8 in the US. Many people are familiar with sage as a culinary herb, but not as medicinal herb.

Make a strong infusion of the fresh or dried herb to spritz or splash the underarms and help control body odor. For best results, make the infusion in the evening and allow to sit overnight before straining. It will need to be applied more frequently than a store bought deodorant, because it will not be as strong. It is not an antiperspirant, either, so it won't keep you dry.

Fresh sage leaves can also be added to an oral hygiene routine with licorice root. Simply rub a fresh sage leaf over the gums and each tooth. Sage has a stronger flavor than licorice, but the leaves can be harvested more often and more easily than licorice roots, making it a good option.

Soapwort, licorice, and sage have many other herbal uses, but they are definitely botanical all-stars when it comes to personal hygiene. Knowing how to grow (speak to someone at your local nursery or do some research on the internet now in order to get these plants growing at home—don't wait!) and use them will mean you always have a backup plan for soap, toothpaste, and deodorant.

8
SANITATION

Sanitation is a dirty-little subject that no one really wants to talk about. It is an often overlooked aspect of emergency preparedness. It is a documented fact that more people die after a disaster due to poor sanitation than from the disaster itself. This is due to individuals not knowing where or how to properly expel waste. Fly infestations also pose a problem, and if waste is left out in the open, then it will only lead to the susceptibility of epidemics such as cholera, typhoid, or giardia.

When a disaster creates a situation where the water sources are compromised, the lack of sanitation in the given disaster area will be a disaster in itself. A 50-mile radius of individuals could be affected by illness and disease. For example, after the 2010 earthquake in Haiti, more than half a million people became ill with cholera due to lack of public sewage systems or sanitary latrines. It became so bad that the disease quickly spread into neighboring countries.

The previous example is one from a known third-world country. This next example is from a first-world country and is more alarming. The 1998, Auckland power crisis was a five-week-long power outage affecting the central city of Auckland, New Zealand. Amongst other grid-down problems, halted water supplies caused a large part of the city's apartment dwellers and office workers to lose the ability to flush their toilets. Only three days into the crisis, (since the average person did not know how to properly deal with their human waste), the resulting lack of wastewater services quickly escalated into a sanitation nightmare. When people were actually confronted with such a situation, they went to the bathroom wherever they could go, filling the toilet, the toilet tank, the tub, the shower, the sink, and when the bathrooms became uninhabitable, they went in corners, boxes, bags, and closets (most, however, left by the time they were using the tub).

As you can see, these are the reasons why you must prepare appropriately for this aspect of a disaster in order to prevent the spread of communicable diseases and downright disgust.

Waste Management
If you can defecate far from your site, that's ideal. If you are in a cramped location, you'll have to manage and dispose of defecation properly or risk disease. If the water system is down or your septic line is clogged, use plastic bags to defecate in. Toilets are sold which attach plastic bags to the seat. Seal them loosely because the gasses will make them expand. Place them in a metal can with a tight lid. This is only a temporary measure. Dig a pit that is a few feet wide and deep. Leave the dirt around the hole so it creates a berm in order to prevent it from becoming flooded. Discard all plastic bags of defecation into the hole and push some dirt over it (don't use the dirt from the berm; dig up dirt from elsewhere). To prevent flies, pests, and other pets, as well as foul odors, pour lime, ash, baking soda, or chlorine bleach into this waste receptacle, and cover with boards.

Add a Sanitation Kit to Disaster Supplies

Having a sanitation kit that is ready in times of disaster is essential to keeping your family and neighbors healthy. These kits can fit comfortably into a bucket, are affordable, and will not take up much space. Additionally, being educated on how to properly dispose of waste is a key factor in keeping everyone safe during a disaster.

Suggested Sanitation-Kit Supplies

- Disposable bucket or Luggable Loo
- Toilet paper
- Rubber gloves
- Garbage bags with twist ties (for liners of toilets or Luggable Loo)
- Bathroom cleaner
- Cat Litter or absorbent material such as saw dust
- Baby wipes
- Hand sanitizer
- Baking soda can be used to help eliminate odors
- Vinegar
- Chlorine bleach
- Shovel

The Cat Hole

In a short-term emergency, a few cat holes will be all that you need. Just take a garden trowel, a small shovel, a post digger, a flat rock, a stick, or anything else that you can find to make a hole approximately 6-8 in. deep and 4-6 in. in diameter. Do your business in the hole, wipe, throw the toilet paper (or leaves) in, and cover it up with the dirt, sand, or snow that you took out.

6-8 in.

Choosing a Site to Bury Waste

- Select a cat hole site far from water sources: 200 feet (approximately 70 adult paces) is the recommended range.
- Select an inconspicuous site untraveled by people. Examples of cat-hole sites include thick undergrowth, near downed timber, or on gentle hillsides.
- If your group is in the same place for more than one night, disperse the cat holes over a wide area; don't go to the same place twice.
- Try to find a site with deep, organic soil. This organic material contains organisms which will help decompose the feces. (Organic soil is usually dark and rich in color.) The desert does not have as much organic soil as a forested area.

- If possible, locate your cat hole where it will receive maximum sunlight. The heat from the sun will aid in decomposition.
- Choose an elevated site where water would not normally runoff during rain storms. The idea here is to keep the feces out of water. Your every thought should be on preventing feces from reaching any water source — be it underground well water, your water table, rivers, lakes, springs, and creeks.
Overtime, the decomposing feces will percolate into the soil before reaching water sources.

So what are some of our options?

- Continue to use the toilet
- The bucket method
- Makeshift latrine (cat hole, latrine trench, straddle trench)

Continue to use the toilet

First off, if you have your own septic system, you're in a better spot over others connected to a town/city sewer line. With a septic system, as long as you have availability to water (from storage or any grey water source—store water in your bathtubs for a short-term solution, when you have advance warning of impending doom), you'll still be able to flush.

If you're connected to a town or city sewer line then the absolute first step is to make sure the sewer main is not down!

If the sewer main is down, don't flush the toilet. Not flushing will prevent your lines from mixing with your neighborhood's "number 2" and backing up into your plumbing (not just the toilets but the sink and tub as well...oh...how gross!).

If you're absolutely sure there is no issue with the sewer lines, then you can follow the same method as someone on a septic system. Just be sure you have enough water for drinking, cleaning, and cooking.

HOW TO FLUSH WITHOUT RUNNING WATER

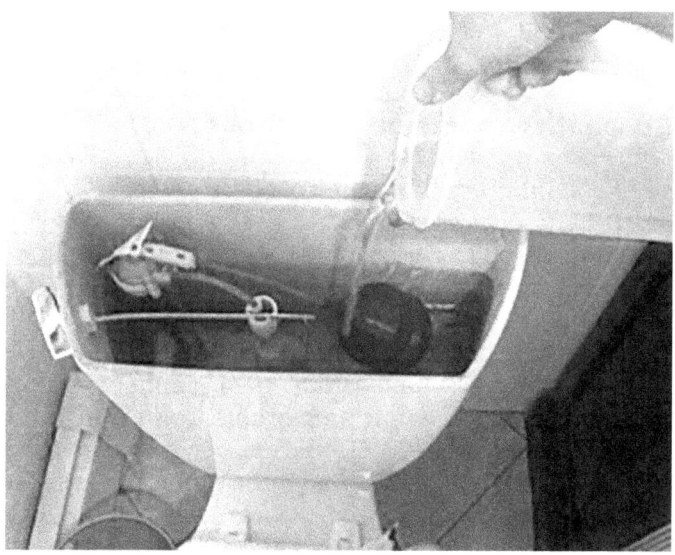

To flush, you can fill up the back tank until the water reaches the float and then hit the flush lever.

If you have a big enough bucket (at least 2 gal.), quickly pour the bucket of water directly in the bowl.

This will trigger the siphoning action and cause it to flush on its own.

Unless we have an ample supply of water, filling the toilet reservoir with water will not be an option. However, with the use of trash bags, we should be able to use the toilet within our home and remove the waste at a later time. The idea here is to place the bag in the toilet, and once we are done, seal the bag until next use.

The average person produces around 2-3 pints of urine and 1 lb. of poop per day. Multiply that by the number of people in your family and in a short time you can only imagine the amount of excrement that would pile up in an extended, grid-down situation in the city.

In most cases, city dwellers (and many suburbanites) do not have access to land where they can safely dig a trench latrine or cat holes. If you are one of these unlucky individuals, you'll need to consider other options. Here are two possibilities that you could use.

USE YOUR EXISTING TOILET

Even if the sewage lines are down or if you're short on water, it's still possible to use your existing toilet.

First, remove as much water as you can from the bowl.

Second, tape a doubled-up trash bag to the underside of the toilet seat and let the bag fill the cavity of the bowl.

Have a pail of wood ash, quicklime, kitty litter, baking soda, or sawdust available so that after each duty is done, the offender can sprinkle a liberal amount over it. This will keep the stench down.

Finally, when the bag is filled up 2/3 the volume of the bowl, add a good amount of quicklime (calcium oxide), wood ash, or other disinfectant. If you do not have any of these things, you can use dirt with a little bit of a chlorine solution sprayed in it. Instead of becoming unnerved by this process, consider this a sort of camping or RV trip. (You could consider stocking up on the chemicals used in RV tanks.)

After the addition of the disinfectant, securely tie up the bag and place it in a temporary, sealable container (like a 5 gal. bucket or trash container). Keep it in there until you can find a good time and place to dispose of it.

Bucket Toilet

There are several options to help us keep the waste either out of the home completely or covered with a lid. One of the advantages of using a bucket is the option of sealing it with a lid. The lid will help keep the smell in and insects out. If a fly gets on the feces and then lands on your food, we could have a recipe for illness.

USE A 5-GAL. BUCKET

A 5 gal. bucket can be used in a similar way to the toilet as previously explained.

Like the toilet method, you'll want to line it with a double-bagged layer of trash bags (heavy duty ones are highly recommended). For a seat, you can either sit on the rim of the bucket directly (it's actually not as uncomfortable as you'd think), place your existing toilet seat on it, or place a couple of 2x4s or other similar objects on the rim to fabricate a makeshift seat.

If you don't mind spending a little money, you can purchase a 5-gallon toilet seat cover, as well as the liners and deodorants for this purpose. The Luggable Loo is a portable, 5-gal., bucket toilet, with seat and snap lid in place. This is probably the easiest way to go (pun intended).

Makeshift Latrine

For a longer-term sanitation solution in rural areas, you'll want to build yourself a trench latrine.

A trench latrine is basically an oversized cat hole that is used multiple times. With the exception of dispersing it over a wide area, the same rules apply to trench latrines as to cat holes.

- Locate the toilet away from food preparation or eating areas.
- Locate latrines and portable toilets at least 200 ft. away from surface-water bodies such as lakes, rivers, streams, and at least 200 ft. downhill or away from any drinking-water source (well or spring), home, apartment, or campsite.
- Provide a place close to the emergency toilet to wash hands that offers soap, running water, and paper towels.

The minimal recommended dimensions are around 1.5 ft. (.45 m) wide x 1 ft. (.3 m) deep x 2 ft. (.6 m) long.

It is also recommended that you build some type of privacy partition. An emergency situation is stressful enough without adding this embarrassment to the mix. Use whatever materials are available to erect a simple partition around your latrine, such as stretching blankets, sheets, or tarps around scrap wood, pipes, poles, etc. Since it is a multi-user station, you'll also want to prevent any flies and pests from coming into contact with the exposed excrement. To do this, after each use cover your business with some wood ash, quick lime, or a few inches of the dirt that came out of the ground when making the pit. I recommend covering with planks in order to prevent pests and pets in and to prevent strong odors from exiting out.

Off-Grid Garbage Disposal

One thing that is not commonly thought of when the grid goes down and services stop running is garbage collection.

If you are like most people who live in a Western society, you probably have a garbage-disposal service that collects your trash weekly. Have you ever thought of what you'd do with your ever growing pile of trash if that service were no longer available?

Not only will the smell be increasingly offensive, but rotting garbage is also a sanitation risk, since it will attract insects and rodents who are vectors of disease. If you have a baby in the house with disposable diapers, you'll only magnify this sanitation risk due to possible fecal-borne diseases.

If you know the grid is likely to be down for a couple of weeks or less, you need not handle your garbage any differently than you currently do. I'm sure many of us have missed a pick-up date or two and had the trash sitting around for a bit without any issues. The problem is when it gets extended to a month or more.

In this case, you'll want to follow a simple, straightforward, 5-step process: sort, dump, drain, burn, or bury.

Sort
The first thing you'll want to do is begin separating the trash into four different groups:

- Biodegradables that decompose quickly (plant & animal matter)
- Paper products
- Plastics and metals (should be flattened or crushed to reduce bulk)
- Sanitary items (diapers, feminine hygiene products, etc.)

Dump

For the biodegradable waste, this can be dumped into a pile or a sturdy container away from your residence.

This will quickly begin to compost and can be used later for gardening.

Drain

After the initial sorting, you'll want to drain off any liquids that are remaining in any containers.

For non-fat liquids, just pour them on the ground. For fatty liquids and oils, pour them into a small "cat hole" that is dug from the ground, and then cover it up with the dirt from the dig. This will prevent the attraction of animals and insects.

Note: Do not add fats and oils to any compost heaps that have been created during the "dump" stage, as this can shut down the composting process.

Burn

Garbage that can be burned (like the paper products that were separated earlier) should be.

If you have the time or inclination, many paper products, like newspapers or junk mail, can be made into serviceable paper logs. These make good sources of fuel for cooking and heating when the grid goes down.

Bury

For the remaining garbage, like metal, glass, plastic, and sanitary items, you'll want to store these for as long as you can in doubled-up trash bags that are in a covered (preferably air-tight) container. However, if the grid is going to be down for a very long time, it may be necessary to bury these.

You'll want to dig a trench or pit that is deep enough so that at least 1 ½ ft. (½ m) of compacted dirt will cover the trash (again, to prevent insects from breeding or animals digging it up). Also, be sure to keep this pit at least 200 ft. from a water source (especially in the case of the sanitary products).

Note: Before burying any items (other than sanitary items, of course), consider how they can be reused, such as using plastic milk jugs to store your water, using glass jars as small containers to store odds and ends, recycling tin cans into mini-planters for nurturing seedlings or for planting seeds, or using a coffee can as a hobo stove. (These are just a few examples out of the multitudes; be creative!)

Fall-Out Shelter Considerations
If you are in a chemical, biological, radiological, or nuclear (CBRN) situation, whereby being forced indoors, many of these outdoor trash disposal solutions will not work for you. In such cases, you'll need to bag and store the waste until you have the opportunity to bury it.

To bag the trash, it's best to first drain off whatever liquid you can and before bagging it, wrap the trash in some type of absorbent material like newspapers or old clothing. This will keep the stench down and hopefully bide you a bit of time before you can dispose of it outdoors.

Summary

As with any emergency plan, don't wait until an emergency to consider making plans. Ask yourself the right questions in order to determine what option/s will work best for you. For instance, what items do you now use that can be turned into recyclables, what kind of toilet system will probably work best for you and your family, where would you bury trash/human waste, etc? Also, determine what supplies you will need now, in order to create an effective toilet system for you and your family in a future, off-grid scenario. Unfortunately, the subject of sanitation is one of the most often ignored parts of a survival plan, yet may instead be one of the most valuable ones.

9
LIGHTING OPTIONS

A fear of the dark is a natural fear and one that nearly all of us experiences to one degree or another from time to time (especially in the case of children).

Perhaps there's good reason for such fears, particularly so during an extended-disaster scenario. Fortunately, most of us have yet to experience prolonged periods of darkness. The most that we've likely experienced is the occasional blackout that lasts for a few hours to a few days (or weeks at most). Most people—even the relatively unprepared—can deal with these situations with a minimal amount of flashlights and batteries, along with candles and matches.

But what happens if those weeks turn into months and those months turn into years? Unless you're REALLY prepared, you're going to end up living in the darkness eventually.

It's ONLY when we experience a true blackout (or seriously remove ourselves from society) that we can even remotely begin to understand what a post-grid, pitch-black scenario might feel like. Granted, we currently have a variety of light sources at our disposal, but there will come a time when they no longer work or we don't have fuel/batteries to run them. Then and only then will we feel the ominous, pitch-black much like our ancestors did.

If you don't already, you need to have back-up lighting for your home, your pack, your vehicle, and your person, so that you won't be hampered in a low- or no-light situation. Light dispels our fears, helps us search for things, and gives us better visibility for certain tasks. There are several low-cost options that we will be discussing that can allow you to see through the darkness when you need it most.

Candles

Candlelight is probably one of the oldest forms of manmade lighting. Candles are simple to use, require no electricity, and there is something special about eating by candlelight. They do have their drawbacks, however. Candles do not give off much light, so you will normally need to use many candles in a room to have any decent lighting. A single candle can light things up enough for walking around and simple tasks, but even reading a book with a single candle can strain one's eyes.

Candles also have a nasty habit of catching things on fire. Obviously, we are talking about an open flame here and candles can catch anything that falls into their path on fire. If you have curtains, for example, that blow open and touch the flame, you could be in for a rude awakening. For this reason, candles should be carefully considered if you desire to use them for your primary lighting needs, and great care should be taken in their use and position in relation to everything else. Children will need strict supervision if using them. Candles also give off smoke, soot, and aren't the cleanest form of light.

There is a triple benefit to using candles, in that they can be used not only for light, but for cooking or warming up food, as well as for heat when cold. Candles can also be made from beeswax. This may not matter to most of us, but for those who keep bees, this will mean that they are set for life in regard to candle-making materials. For those of us that aren't beekeepers, start stocking-up beeswax that can be used for this purpose in the future. Beeswax sheets can be stored easily and compactly, rather than storing full-length candles.

In our house we have a few different candle options. When I started prepping, I was out at the grocery store one day and saw the big, 7-day, pillar-jar, saint candles that Catholics traditionally use for their altars and rituals. Being Protestant, I decided to disregard their use as religious relics and instead use them for survival preparations. I quickly bought these for back-up light, as they are quite inexpensive, considering that each candle will last for 7 days. I then went to Wal-Mart and bought decorative candles about the size of a coke can. Lastly, I found a seller off *eBay* that sells candles in bulk, and I got a whole box of 15-hour candles. Box a variety of candles along with the rest of your supplies.

Oil, Propane, and Kerosene Lanterns
For me, lanterns make the most sense for a heavy-duty light, but they are not without issues either. There are a few different types of lanterns that I have or have considered for light if the power goes out. The first type is the old-fashioned oil lamps that you can get from a lot of places like Amazon. Actually, now that I look at the prices again, they have come down and there are a lot of good options for oil lamps on this website. Oil lamps give

off much more light than a candle and have a sturdier base. If you have a reflector, the light is magnified slightly and makes a better choice for a whole-room light. Also, with oil lamps, you can walk around a bit easier, since most have a guard over the flame to prevent wind from blowing directly on the light.

Just like with candles, oil lamps are potentially dangerous if they are dropped or if the flame touches something else. I would recommend their use in situations where children aren't involved or where great care is taken when using them. I know they have been used for millennia, but they have also probably started fires for millennia, so just a simple word of caution.

Propane lanterns are incredible. I have one that I use for camping and as a back-up for power outages. The light these things put out is incredible, and you can even cook on them, yes, they get that hot! Just remember, propane needs to be vented, so you don't want to use a propane lantern in your house without proper ventilation. I have purchased a good amount of additional propane cylinders and mantle wicks that I can use for a very long time, if needed. This style of lamp is my ideal, dual-purpose light. It is safe enough to use (with those exceptions mentioned) if your power goes out or if you are out in the woods.

Kerosene lanterns are another good option, but they, like propane, need to be vented. These too are abundant at estate sales where they can be picked up very economically. In addition to kerosene, they will also burn lantern oil, which comes in plastic bottles. Lantern oil is more refined and burns cleaner but is much more expensive and some complain that it does not wick as well as kerosene. If you plan on using kerosene lanterns you will want to store a supply of kerosene, extra mantles or wicks, and extra globes in case yours breaks. Kerosene will keep longer than gasoline, but try to rotate it out every few years or so. If you also have a kerosene heater you can burn your kerosene during the cold months each year so you can replace your supply with fresh stock.

With any type of flame-based lighting, it is important to have proper fire extinguishing equipment close at hand in case of any accidents. I would never recommend leaving these lit while asleep.

Flashlights
Flashlights come in all flavors and sizes. I have a couple of different options for the different uses that each one needs to fill.

For hands-free operation, I must recommend the headlight. Headlights have been around for years in various configurations. You might have the image of a coal-coated miner from a bygone era, walking around with that big light, strapped to his helmet. They have come a very long way since those days.

Headlights are now extremely light, and much more powerful, thanks to LED light bulbs. I have Petzl headlamps for everyone in my family, and they have been perfect for mulling around the campground at night or for evening hikes. Most use 3 AAA batteries so that you aren't stuck with something that requires hard-to-find batteries. The ones I have adjust the tilt so you can easily shine the light on your lap if you want to see what you are eating or out ahead to light up the trail as you are walking. They also have three modes: low, high, and strobe for different lighting situations.

They are held in front of your head by a comfortable, elastic-type band that isn't too tight and is easily adjustable. Not only are headlights good for camping and hikes, but also for long car trips; if I have to change a tire in the middle of the night, I need both hands free. Headlamps are also nice to use for around-the-house chores when either more light is needed or for when the power goes out. When not in use, simply pull them down around your neck. For ambient lighting, take them off and shine them at the ceiling.

Regular, hand-held flashlights certainly have their place as well, and our family has several different types and styles of these. A good place to purchase LED flashlights, at a very affordable price, is at Costco. Often times they come in packs of three and have the batteries included for each flashlight, with great illumination of over 200 lumens. They are cheap enough to have in most rooms of your home. I have an unopened three pack I keep in the trunk of my car, so I'm covered pretty much at all times.

Beware of the solar flashlights, for the most part. Yes, they may be handy and user friendly, but they are not going to give the illumination that standard flashlights are going to give. That being said, the only one that I highly recommend in this category is the Goal Zero Portable Torch 250 with Power Hub and Emergency Light with Solar and Hand Crank. Boasting a powerful, 4,400-mAh-lithium battery, 250-total-lumen output, a 1.5A USB port to charge your gear, as well as a built-in solar panel and hand crank, this multi-function flashlight creates bright light anywhere.

Batteries are an important consideration, I'll admit, with flashlights, but you can purchase rechargeable batteries and a foldable, solar-panel-charging system, like the Goal Zero Guide 10 Plus Solar Recharging Kit, to keep you supplied with plenty of light for a long time.

Light Sticks
Light sticks are chemiluminescent substances in plastic tubes that provide hours of illumination in a number of safety, industrial, and military applications. Light sticks are waterproof, non-flammable, and non-sparking, which makes them useful in hazardous situations where sparks or flame could cause an explosion. Duration is determined by the chemistry of the formulation. Brightness is affected by temperature: the warmer the temperature, the brighter the light will appear. Viewing distance can be affected by temperature,

moisture, and other elements. Exposure to direct sunlight can reduce shelf life and effectiveness.

I have tried a few different brands and my favorite so far is the Cyalume SnapLight. It is a very bright light, providing instant 360-degree illumination that can be seen up to a mile away for up to 12 hours in optimal conditions. To activate the light stick, bend, snap, and shake the tube. The light stick has a hook and gate top, for hanging or attaching. Each light stick is individually foil-wrapped for protection from light and moisture and has up to a five-year shelf life from date of manufacture. Stay away from generic ones that are sold around Halloween; there is a massive difference when you compare those with military-grade ones.

Self-Contained, Solar-Powered Lights

When talking about self-contained, solar-panel lights, there is quite a variety to choose from. They run the gamut from small, cheap, plastic, inexpensive, landscape lighting to bright, high-powered solar-street lights. Unfortunately, there is a growing group of novice preppers who seem to think their solar-powered garden lights will light their way in times of calamity. Yes, there are some creative uses for these lights, especially in a pinch, but consider the fact that they barely give off more light then the screen of your cellphone. If you are going to spend the money, save up for something that is less likely to break and frustrate and more likely to satisfy.

Hand Crank

I am sure most of you have seen the hand-cranked flashlights for sale. These have a small motor that is activated when you either crank a handle like a fishing rod or squeeze a lever like a stress ball for a long time. These sounded great to me when I first heard about them, but after trying to use these several times, I decided that they aren't going to work for me. I am all for exercise, but not when I need light. When it counts, I want bright light that can help me see what I am looking for, or illuminate what I am trying to do. The hand-crank lights are novelties that just aren't the best solution.

Goal Zero Lighthouse Lantern

I know I said to basically not waste your time with any light source that has solar and handcrank power for illumination, but there are always exceptions to the rules, and this is a big one. If I had the money I would buy 10 more of them! The Lighthouse Lantern from Goal Zero is the epitome of emergency preparedness and the perfect light for any back-up kit. Light up any situation with 250 lumens of bright, LED light or use the dimmable, DuaLite Directional Lighting feature to save on power for extended runtime. All in all, it's the only light you'll ever need.

Traditional, battery-powered lanterns rely on costly D batteries that can leave you left in the dark if you're not prepared. I don't know about you, but I'm pretty sick of batteries for powering light sources (unless they are for back-up lighting that is going to be used infrequently). They are expensive, dead when you need them most, and once they are gone, so is your light.

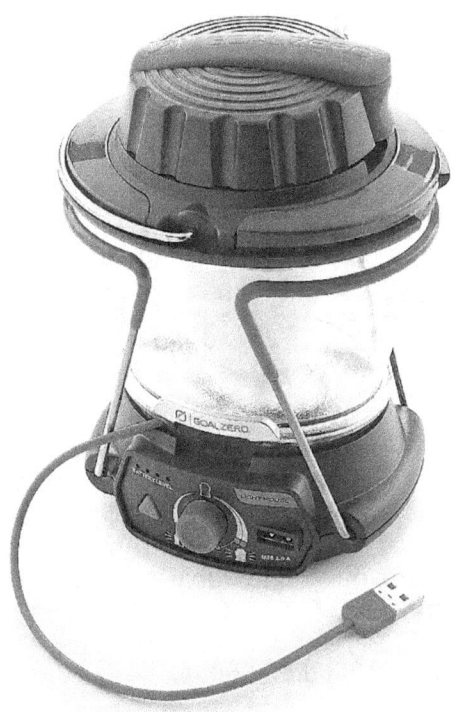

There are a few amazing ways to charge the Lighthouse Lantern:

The Sun
The Lighthouse can be charged by connecting a compatible solar panel.

USB
The Lighthouse Lantern can also be charged by being plugged into a USB power source.

Hand Crank
When you are really in a pinch, use the hand crank to get 10 mins of light for every 1 minute of cranking.

USB Rechargeable Flashlights
Rechargeable LED flashlights are finally gaining popularity. Most have a built-in, micro-USB port, like cellphones, so they can be conveniently recharged with a wall-outlet, charging plug, power pack, or compatible solar panel—again, no more batteries to weigh down my pack and leak and die or end up being the wrong size. I've seen rechargeable, LED-flashlight models recently that have 900+ lumens on their highest output setting and will run 28+ hours on their lowest setting.

I have switched all of my illumination and devices to run only on rechargeable batteries (at least these can be reused, so no need for multiple sets) that can be recharged by portable, solar means. When I'm out walking or hiking in the hills during the day, I just hang a foldable solar panel from the back of my pack (Goal Zero Guide 10 Plus Solar Recharging Kit) and keep my flashlight and smartphone going indefinitely. You can place this foldable solar panel anywhere: the dashboard of your car while driving, your window sill, lying next to you while you sunbathe, etc.

The light sticks make a good backup, and you should still stock up on some normal, common-size batteries for a rainy day.

I can't stress enough that any light source is better than no light source at all. Make sure you have some means ready to go at all times! I can't tell you how many times I have left my $100, super-bright, Surefire light at home and had to work on something at night with only the moonlight—pretty embarrassing to ask friends or family for a flashlight when you claim to know so much about urban survival.

Makeshift, Urban-Survival Lights

It's impossible to be perfectly prepared for an imperfect world. Sometimes you just have to go MacGyver and solve common problems by using the resources you have on hand and a little bit of ingenuity. I've always said that the ability to improvise is one of the most important survival skills.

This section is a collection (not all my own I'll admit) of a few creative, makeshift-lighting solutions you may have to deploy as a last resort if the grid goes down. You just never know when one of these innovative ideas might shed some light into your darkness.

Shining Sardines

Sardines are an excellent survival food. They have a long shelf-life and are full of protein and fats. Maybe you have some sardines packed in your emergency-food storage. If not, consider them.

Oil lamps have been used for thousands of years. From olive oil to rendered whale blubber to modern kerosene lanterns, oil lamps are excellent, off-grid-lighting solutions. What do sardines, tuna, anchovies, and oil lamps have in common? They have quite a lot, actually, if they are all packed in olive oil.

Once you're done munching on those tasty bites of fish, place a natural-fiber wick into the remaining oil and slightly over the edge of the sardine container. The wick, in this case a cotton string from a mop head, will absorb the oil. Once the wick is fully soaked, simply light the end. A sardine lamp with just a little bit of oil will burn for many hours. Sure, it'll smell like fish, but that's what you get for not including emergency candles in your "bug-in" supplies. Are you running low on oil? No problem, just top it off with some more olive oil from the pantry—or any cooking oil for that matter.

Glowing Crayons

Games and toys are excellent items to pack in an emergency kit, especially if you have small children. Simple toys such as crayons and coloring books can help keep their mind off of the misfortune that caused the lights to go out in the first place.

If you have focused only on toys and not on the essentials, like candles and flashlights, you may have to sacrifice some of your children's least favorite crayon colors and make some "crayndles" (a new coined word to add to the urban dictionary). Crayons are basically colored wax. If you're in a hurry, just break the point off and light the paper label at the end of the crayon. As the wax melts, the paper becomes a "wick." One "crayndle" will last you for about 30 minutes.

You can also get a little more creative and sandwich a natural fiber wick (like a shred of t-shirt material) between three crayons that have been stripped of their labels. Bind everything together with two short pieces of wire (paper clips work well), then simply light the wick. Mine usually burn for an hour. That's not too bad for a 10-second, makeshift "crayndle."

Blazing Bottles

If you've listened to anything that I said in Build the Perfect Bug Out Bag, then I know you at least have a headlamp packed in your 72-hour-disaster kit.

Yet as nice as headlamps are, they aren't always the perfect lighting solution. Ever tried having dinner or playing cards across the table with someone who's wearing a headlamp flashlight? It's really annoying and gets really old, really fast. You get blinded every time they look at you.

Instead, set a relaxing mood that's perfect for cards and a sardine dinner using a headlamp and a water-filled clear plastic gallon jug (or any clear container filled with water). Invert the headlamp around the bottle so that the light shines toward the CENTER of the bottle. The water diffuses and diverts the light, making a nice, mellow, glowing lamp that will help set a perfect mood during any disaster "bug in."

Beaconing Bacon

Do you have a jar in the cupboard where you pour and keep excess bacon grease? This grease makes the perfect, improvised survival candle. Jam in a natural fiber wick and light. It'll burn as long as any comparably-sized candle. See this post about how to make a bacon-grease candle.

No bacon grease? No problem. If the electricity is out, then the bacon in the fridge is going to go bad anyway, so you might as well use it for something. Tear off the fatty pieces and jam them in a jar around a natural fiber wick, and this will burn like a candle as well. The fatty bacon pieces will melt just like wax. Mmmmm, smells like bacon. TIP: Smear the wick with bacon fat first!

Kindling Crisco

What if the electricity is off for more than 30 days straight and you need a light source that will shine for at least one month? That's no problem, Crisco has you covered.

Press a natural-fiber wick (like a cotton t-shirt shred or a mop strand), using a forked stick, all the way to the bottom of a can of Crisco, and you will have one of the longest-burning, emergency candles on the planet. Smear the top of the wick with Crisco to help it burn better. I've heard reports of these burning for more than 30 days straight!

Conclusion

What's the lesson here? Make sure you have non-electric lighting solutions in place, just in case the grid goes down. If your solutions are battery powered, you will need to store extra batteries as well. Oil lamps, flashlights, candles, and glow sticks are great emergency-light sources. Don't resort to smashing bacon fat into a jar with your bare hands unless you absolutely have to.

Note: Candles have a bad reputation of causing house fires. Makeshift, improvised candles are even more dangerous. Use these only as a last resort, burn them only on a non-combustible surface and keep close watch on any makeshift candle. A house fire can turn a "bug in" scenario into a "bug out" scenario really fast.

10
ALTERNATIVE POWER SOURCES

One of the biggest concerns when considering a collapse of the infrastructure is how people with no electricity, especially in an urban environment, will react and survive. Those who are moving to retreat properties make it a point to look for land with its own source of fuel in order to accommodate future fuel needs. Whether those sources are an ample wood supply, a natural gas well, or a surface coal seam, these resources ensure continual power for their home and their equipment.

Without these resources readily available, stored-fuel sources will eventually run out. A way to avoid this future crisis is to consider investing in devices that collect renewable energy in order to supply homes and retreats with a persistent supply of power.

Generators

Generators are great for short-term power outages. They are relatively cheap and can be sourced from most home-improvement stores. If the grid goes down for a few days after a major storm, generators will keep the food in the fridge from spoiling, keep the sump pump running, and make sure a few lights stay on inside the home. However, for long-term, grid-down outages, generators should not be counted on to provide life-sustaining support.

Fuel Availability

With the exception of solar-powered generators, all generators run on some sort of fuel (gasoline, diesel, propane, and natural gas). After Hurricane Sandy hit the East Coast, fuel shortages were immediate and widespread. Now, let's imagine a large-scale power outage occurring over a prolonged period of time? Gasoline and diesel will not be available for purchase from local stations and any that happens to be on hand will most likely go to emergency vehicles first. Propane will be long gone at the local hardware store (it was all sold out prior to Hurricane Sandy even hitting in some areas). Generators powered by natural gas will initially be immune to this, but will soon face their own shortcomings.

Fuel-Storage Considerations

Most portable generators use 8-22 gal. of gasoline per day, compared to 4-8, 20 lb. propane tanks (for propane generators). That's quite a bit of fuel just for one day's usage. It's simply not realistic to assume that the average person will be able to store enough fuel on site to keep the generator running for weeks on end. At 15 gal. of gasoline per day, that equates to keeping 42, 5 gal. gas containers on hand to power the generator for 2 weeks. Even a large, 250-gal. propane tank only has 3-4 weeks' worth of fuel, if that. That's hardly enough to keep the lights on during a long-term, grid-down scenario, wouldn't you say.

Operational Security (OPSEC)

Let's consider the security aspects that come along with using a generator for long-term. You probably know where I am going with this. Even if you could miraculously keep your generator running long after the apocalypse, you would only succeed in making yourself a colossal target (unless, maybe, you live out in the country).

This doesn't mean that you should be discouraged in using a generator for short-term use. Generators play a huge role in keeping people comfortable when storms like Hurricane Sandy pummel an area. All you need to understand is that there are shortcomings associated with generators and that in a long-term, grid-down scenario, these devices should not be part of your overall survival plan.

Batteries

Most of our emergency devices require batteries and having an abundance of them with the capability of being recharged is a very good investment. The best batteries on the market right now are NiMH (nickel-metal hydride) that have a low self-discharge (LSD). To prolong the charge of your batteries, store them in a sealed bag in the back of your refrigerator. This prevents condensation and extends the life of the battery.

Also, consider purchasing lead-acid, deep-cycle, direct current (DC) batteries (also called solar batteries). Solar batteries provide energy storage for solar, wind, and other renewable energy systems. Different from a car battery, a deep-cycle battery is capable of surviving prolonged, repeated, and deep discharges which are typical in renewable energy systems that are off grid. Having multiple DC batteries hooked up and working together creates a battery bank and allows you to run more of your household appliances using solar energy. Deep-cycle batteries can be a large expense for a sizable, off-grid system, but with proper care and maintenance, they should last 5-10 years.

Solar Energy

Harnessing the sun's magnificent power has become quite the craze lately. In some states, having photovoltaic panels can make you eligible for a 30% federal tax credit!

A solar-power system has three components: solar panel(s), charge controller, and batteries. As the sun's rays hit the solar cells on a photovoltaic (PV) panel, the power is transferred to a silicon semiconductor. The power is then changed into direct-current (DC) electricity and passed through connecting wires to enter a storage battery.

- **Solar panels** come in all different shapes and sizes. If you are considering purchasing some supplies for solar power, consider first starting out with a basic set and then adding additional items to the existing set.

- **Solar generators** have many advantages. A few being that they don't produce dangerous fumes, they run quietly, they are energy efficient, and no fuel is required to run them. The best part is that these generators can last for 25 years or longer! Although the initial expense can be high, there is no additional cost to run the generator, so it's a great investment. For that matter, who says that a solar generator can only be used during disasters? Running your solar generator regularly will keep your electricity bills down. Consider the Goal Zero Yeti 1250 Kit. It is a well-established model and is fairly inexpensive for what it is.

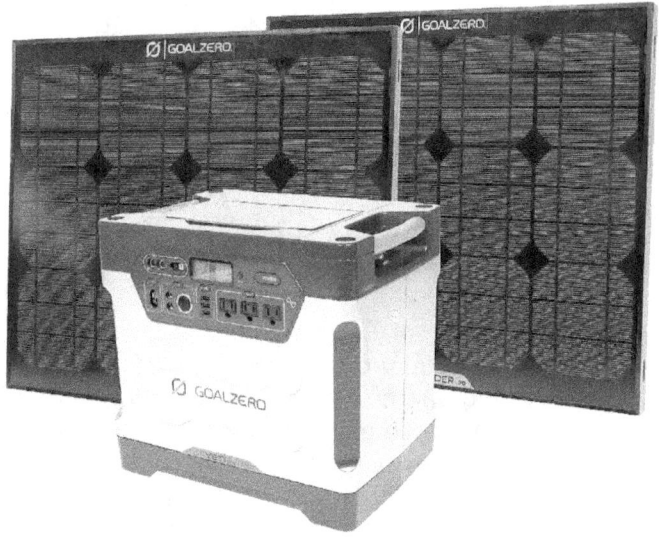

- **Mobile, solar-power systems** would be ideal for bug-out bags. Keep in mind that these systems can easily be stolen, hence the term "portable, solar-power systems." They should be placed in a secure, well-guarded area.

The Goal Zero Sherpa 50 Solar Recharging Kit and Power Inverter offer a versatile, go-anywhere, power source that charges USB-, 12V-, and alternating current (AC) devices such as laptops, tablets, e-readers, and smartphones.

- **Solar-battery chargers** use trickle charging and can be somewhat time consuming. To expedite the process, many preppers buy two or three chargers to use simultaneously. However, there are solar chargers that can be connected to a photovoltaic (PV) panel and can make a huge difference in recharging batteries and providing power to small-scale appliances. Those that live in humid or rainy environments may want to consider a charger that is weather resistant. Lastly, ensure your solar-battery charger can charge a variety of battery sizes and has smart capability.

Inverters

An inverter is an electronic device that converts DC power into AC power. Ensure that you find an inverter that can handle your initial and anticipated needs. You can figure out the wattage by looking at the manufacture's label on the appliance or by using the amps listed. Use the following formula to convert amps into watts: amps x 115 volts=wattage.

Natural-Power Sources

The power from wind and water has been used for centuries and can easily be adopted to fit most self-reliant lifestyles.

- **Wind** energy can be harnessed by mounting wind turbines in high locations such as on rooftops. (Having a professional mount the turbine would be beneficial.) Many preppers do not recommend wind turbines because of their high maintenance and the risks associated with tower climbing. However, if you happen to live in an area that is very windy, with lots of cloud coverage, it could be a suitable option, although a dangerous one.

- **Water** energy has a lot of power. Anyone who has seen Niagara Falls knows what I'm talking about! Steep parcels of land with large creeks running through them can be ideal spots for water turbines. A water turbine or hydro generator has the capacity of producing 10 amps around the clock and matches the usable power generated by over 40 amps of solar modules. The power system itself is the same as solar, except that only diversion-type, charge controls can be used with hydro.

There are many reasons to invest in alternate power sources. If the subject of peak oil isn't enough, consider the fragility of the grid. As it stands, our country cannot exist without the electrical grid, and sometime in the not-so-distant future our lives could change drastically by a single event or disaster. While there is no way to predict when this will happen, we would be wise to prepare for this certainty.

Preps to Buy

- Rechargeable batteries in assorted sizes and in bulk
- DC batteries in bulk
- Solar-battery chargers
- Solar, photovoltaic (PV) panel (5 watts or more)
- Generator (solar-powered, diesel-run generators are preferable). Also, keep in mind that a typical size for a home-backup generator is 4,500 watts continuous and 5,500 watts peak.)
- Inverter
- Extra parts for any alternative energy equipment and generators
- Extra-fuel sources you regularly use (propane, gasoline, diesel, etc.)
- Fuel stabilizers if using gasoline (such as Sta-bil) or if using diesel, have a ready supply of diesel-fuel supplements to prevent gelling and a diesel, antibacterial additive to prevent both growth and gelling.

Action to take

- Make a spreadsheet of the total wattage the household uses.

- Do your homework. Only purchase alternative-power-supply devices that are compatible with your needs.
- Ensure that your equipment is kept securely. Hardened, bolt-cutter-resistant security chains and a padlock can do wonders!
- When using any alternative power supply, monitor your supply to ensure that the power is sufficient for your needs.

11
LOOTING VS. SCAVENGING

Before we can truly and fully discuss the permissibility of looting and/or scavenging, we must first know and understand the exact definition of each word, as well as recognize the differences between the two in a real-life setting.

Merriam-Webster defines the verb loot as follows:

- To steal things from (a place, such as a store or house) during a war or after destruction has been caused by fire, rioting, etc.
- To plunder or sack in war
- To rob especially on a large scale and usually by violence or corruption
- To seize and carry away by force especially in war
- To engage in robbing or plundering especially in war
- The soldiers were looting every house that they came to (example).
- Soldiers swept through the territory, looting, burning, and killing (example).

As you can see, the term looting is essentially synonymous with stealing, plundering, sacking, robbing, and seizing, often with violence or corruption.

Now, let's see how Merriam-Webster defines the word scavenge:

- To search through waste, junk, etc., for something that can be saved or used
- To salvage from discarded or refuse material; also: to salvage usable material from
- He scavenged the town dump for automobile parts (example).

With these terms now defined properly and in context, we can dialogue as to what is morally permissible in regard to them both.

To come to any sensible conclusion, facts must be gathered and categorized into a logical sequence. Let's consider the "Five Ws" (and one H), which were memorialized by Rudyard Kipling in his Just So Stories (1902), in which a poem accompanying the tale of "The Elephant's Child" opens with:

I keep six honest serving-men
(They taught me all I knew);
Their names are What and Why and When
And How and Where and Who.

This is why the "Five Ws and One H" problem-solving method is also called the "Kipling Method," which helps to explore problems by challenging them with these questions.

The Five Ws, Five Ws and one H, or the Six Ws are questions whose answers are considered basic in information-gathering. They are often mentioned in journalism (cf. news style), research, and police investigations. They constitute a formula for getting the complete story on a subject. According to the principle of the Five Ws, a report can only be considered complete if it answers the:

- Who?
- What?
- When?
- Where?
- Why?

Some authors add a sixth question, "how," to the list, though "how" can also be covered by "what," "when," or "where."

Each question should have a factual answer — facts necessary to include for a report to be considered complete. Importantly, none of these questions can be answered with a simple "yes" or "no".

OK, let's get started by asking the "who" question. Who is "taking" and who is "being taking from"? In a survival situation, these are people who are either in need or are in want. The person in need may be someone who has run out of food, shelter, clothing, etc. Maybe his or her baby has no more formula, diapers, or wet wipes. Maybe there is no more fire wood or the last of the ammunition has been used. A person in want would be someone who has what is needed in order to live, but wants to take advantage of the situation by stealing impractical or unnecessary items. The "wanted" or "needed" items could be taken from a variety of places, such as stores, warehouses, homes, stranded vehicles, factories, businesses, banks, etc.

What is being taken? Is it something needed to sustain life or is it simply wanted because of monetary value or because of the novelty of it? I will name items below and classify them as either "wants" or "needs."

- Flat-screen TV: want
- DVD player: want
- Stereo: want
- Jewelry: want
- Perfume/cologne: want
- Nail polish: want
- Hair dye: want
- Furniture: want
- Computer/laptop: want
- Home décor: want
- Collectables: want
- Water: need
- Canned food: need
- Baby formula: need
- Diapers: need
- Jackets, socks, boots in the winter: need
- Medicine: need
- Sanitary supplies, i.e., toilet paper, feminine napkins, etc.: need
- Gasoline for your escape-vehicle: need

- Fire wood and matches: need
- Family-sized tent (i.e. if house burned-down): need
- Ammunition for hunting or for self-defense: need

What is the setting (when and where) of this theoretical drama? The answer to the "when" question is whenever a survival situation presents itself, and the answer to the "where" question depends on if this catastrophe will occur on a local, regional, national, or international level.

"Why" are the items being taken? Are they being sought after because they are "needed" or because they are "wanted?" Do they just have monetary value or do they have life-sustaining value? Are they simply pretty or practical? I suppose anyone can justify anything when conscience is set aside, but in general, assuming you are a God-loving, morally-driven humanitarian, these questions should be relatively easy to answer.

"How" are these things being procured? Are they being taken by force? Is a gun being put to someone's head? Is someone crying in fear at your presence? Is there a physical owner present or refusing that you take whatever you long for, whether it be out of necessity or greed?

By answering all of these questions, we are now able to put some scenarios into place. We can now use our conscience radar to determine right from wrong.

In San Francisco, following the horrific earthquake that befell the city in 1906, the police behaved pretty well, but then the U.S. Army marched in and imposed its own version of order. One man was bayoneted by a soldier after taking supplies at the invitation of the proprietor of a grocery doomed to burn. A bank cashier was shot trying to open his own bank's safe. A man trying to rescue someone trapped in the rubble was shot dead after being mistaken for a looter. Estimates of those killed by the authorities run as high as 500, but actual numbers will never be known, because the bodies of the killed were thrown into the flames and the bay. Obviously, what these individuals did was COMPLETELY justifiable and the ARMY essentially imposed capital punishment indiscriminately. These San Franciscons were neither scavengers nor looters, but were certainly treated as such by the Army.

In New Orleans, following Hurricane Katrina, around the corner on Canal Street, the main thoroughfare in the central business district, people sloshed headlong through hip-deep water as individuals ripped open the steel gates on the front of several clothing and jewelry stores. One man, who had about 10 pairs of jeans draped over his left arm, was asked if he was salvaging things from his store. "No," the man shouted, "that's everybody's store." People filled industrial-sized garbage cans with clothing and jewelry and floated them down the street on bits of plywood and insulation as National Guard lumbered by. One man with an armload of clothes even asked a policeman, "Can I borrow your car?" Without question, these are examples of looting. These New Orleanians took advantage of a moment in time without rule of law. Did these individuals really need to steel clothing and jewelry? Were these things needed for survival? These acts surely were acts of looting.

Again, following Hurricane Katrina, another incident unfolded, but of a different nature. At a drug store on Canal Street, just outside the French Quarter, two police officers with pump shotguns stood guard as workers from the Ritz-Carlton Hotel across the street loaded large laundry bins full of medications, snack foods, and bottled water. "This is for the sick," Officer Jeff Jacob said. "We can commandeer whatever we see fit, whatever is necessary to maintain law." Another officer, D.J. Butler, told the crowd standing around that they would be out of the way as soon as they got the necessities. "I'm not saying you're welcome to it," the officer said. "This is the situation we're in. We have to make the best of it." In my opinion, whether these goods had been taken by common citizens or by the police, they would have still been taken for a good cause. Would this be considered looting or scavenging? Well, I suppose this would, by definition, be looting, however, I think it could be treated as scavenging, as these items were needed and couldn't be obtained any other way.

As you can see, different possibilities will play-out after a calamity, and you must ask God to aid you in making the determination as to what is or is not morally acceptable.

The rest of the chapter will examine how to safely, and in an organized fashion, scavenge after a presumed, long-term crisis. We will also contemplate what items will need to be salvaged during a "scavenger hunt."

The Threat from Scavenging

Scavenging will most likely require your survival group to visit highways, population centers, government facilities, farms, and other installations. Each mission must be evaluated. Prior to a scavenging operation, a scout should be sent out equipped with a direct line of communication to your base of operations. Scouts should be fully versed in travelling through hostile territories, preventing a hostile force from tracking your scout back to your base. Service members who were infantry in the military are ideal scouts. They are well-trained, well-disciplined, and an essential element of your survival group.

Scouts should survey the target area from a safe distance using standard surveillance techniques to avoid detection. Such evaluations should consider hostile, occupying force, environmental-risk (chemical, biological, radiological, nuclear, and natural conditions) variables, and operational costs. Operational costs include: distance, weather conditions, and force elimination. By establishing operational costs, the scout can report to the commander of the survival group, outlining how much food, water, fuel, required equipment, force, and munitions the scavenging operation will cost, at which time the commander can make the call.

If it's not worth it, it's not worth it! Should your commander make the decision to carry out the operation, those assigned to carry out the task must be well versed in combat and tactical operations. Scavenging, like all other ops, must maintain command, control, communications, and intelligence.

Where to Scavenge

Your scavenging target shouldn't be some random location like Wal-Mart; your target should fit your need. Going to a random location with no direction would likely force your group into a compromised situation. Aimlessly moving from one location to the next is strictly prohibited. It's prohibited because it will drain your group while exposing them to human and natural threats.

Scavenging operations should not only have a specific target, but two backup targets should be established (when applicable). The following are examples of scavenging needs and their targets.

Automotive Parts

Logic would dictate that the last place looted would be automotive shops. I don't see a Mad Max scenario happening, because most of today's generation can't even change a tire. In the absence of an automotive shop, you will need to scavenge from nearby, abandoned vehicles. Luckily, a part replacement, scavenge op will most likely only need a three-man team: two assisting cover and a mechanic who will know what types of automotive parts are needed.

Renewable Power

Again, this could easily be considered a low-risk op with a three-man team. Excellent locations include federal installations. Federal installations are equipped with commercial-grade solar panels. Such locations include: power-substations, federal office buildings, freeway lighting, etc.

Fuel

Fuel can be scavenged from abandoned vehicles by siphoning gas from: abandoned tankers (if operable, better to take the tanker), cars/trucks, convenience-store fuel holds, etc. You will need a vehicle to transport the fuel when applicable and a four-man team to acquire it.

Ammunition

Had you taken the often given advice from preppers, you'd probably be reloading your own ammo. Even then, you could potentially run out of ammo. In this event, you would have to take on a high-risk op. Ammo will be a hard thing to come by, and in the event of scavenging for ammo, you will need a five-man team. Five are required, not only for adequate force, but for adequate manpower. Ammo is heavy! Such targets include: military bases, law-enforcement vehicles and stations, gun stores, and dead bodies.

Food and Water

Food and water will be extremely hard to come by when scavenging (food more so than water, in most locations). Think unconventionally. For food, target wholesale-distribution warehouses. You will have to establish these locations prior to disaster, because they are not easily identified. In addition to distribution centers, food can be acquired from: abandoned homes, tractor trailers, grain mills, farms, etc.

Niceties and Necessities

Niceties and necessities include various items that make survival much more tolerable. Necessities include: birth control, prophylactics, bleach, soaps, detergents, etc. Niceties include: entertainment, board games, toys for the kids, electronics, etc. Birth control is a priority. Pregnancy after without rule of law will not be easy! However, if a member of your group becomes pregnant, that child is not only the mother's responsibility, but the entire group's. Children take priority over all.

The acquisition of these items should not take precedent over the safety of the group. These items can be acquired from several locations; you just have to be smart.

Mapping Your List
Get a detailed map of your city and mark off potential scavenging locations. Make a legend with symbols to represent different types of locations: (for instance) use a circle for food stores, triangles for hunting/outdoor stores, squares for hospitals and pharmacies, etc. A good resource for finding addresses and locations is Google maps. Just type in a store name and Google will give you all the addresses for that store in your area. Copy and paste the results into a .txt file and print it out for future reference. This map is extremely important and should be kept in a safe place. The map should be copied and distributed among friends and family members. Here is a list of some locations to keep in mind:

- Hospitals/Pharmacies
- Restaurants
- Grocery stores
- Large stores and warehouses
- Police/Fire stations
- Factories
- Shipyards/ Shipping-container sites
- Liquor stores
- Shopping malls

- Hotels
- Schools
- Sporting-goods stores
- Outdoor-living stores
- Garden stores
- Hardware stores
- Military/Armory bases
- Gas stations
- Airports

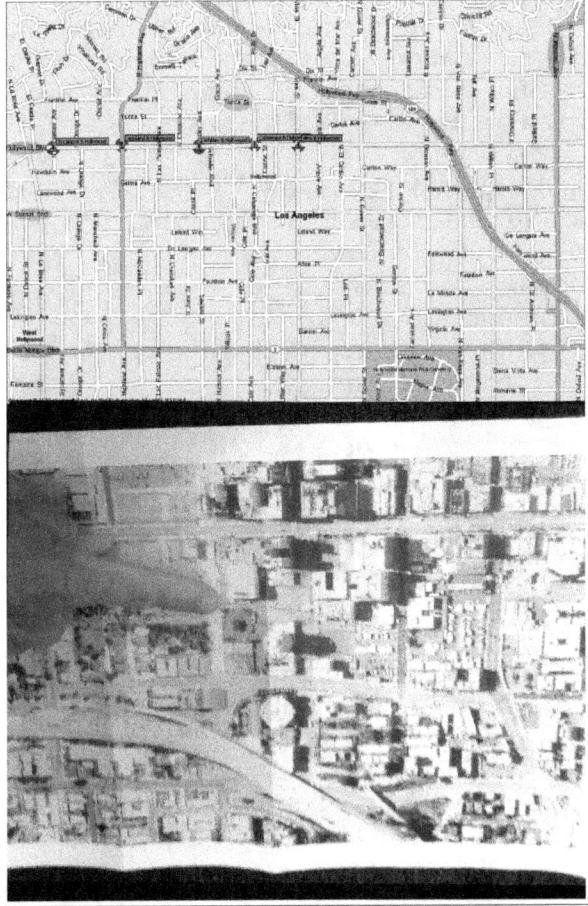

12
L.A.S.T O.U.T

The Last One Out
The journey for most will be long and treacherous, and may take days, weeks, months, or even years. This will result in injuries and casualties along the way, however, those who are prepared, trained, and have an up-to-date evacuation plan, with a viable destination, will have the potential to be successful. This chapter will help you create a bug-out plan by covering all of the basics.

Bugging-out may be one of the most discussed topics in the survival and preparedness world, topped only by everyone's favorite genre—firearms. Every day there are new articles about bugging-out, with everything from the "must have" BOB, to the most dependable fire starter, to the best communications gear, to the brightest flashlight, to the most accurate compass, and more, but rarely does the topic of evacuation planning and most desirable destination come to the forefront of the discussions. Why? It's just not as exciting and most folks simply think they can make up a route as they go along.

The Bug-Out "Dream"
You have bought a large plot of land halfway across the country with all of your closest friends. You have the coolest bug-out bags ever conceived and are waiting for the inevitable mushroom cloud to appear. One day, it happens! In a magnificently coordinated evacuation plan, every one's 4x4s drive-off into the sunset, arriving unscathed at a

fully-stocked, self-sustaining retreat a few days later, having fought through several heavily-armed roadblocks, while dodging every bullet, dressed like marines fighting in Fallujah. All of you survive, just like you pictured it, and all ends well. The rest of the world is in ruins, but your group is finally safe and will survive for generations to come.

The Gut-Wrenching Reality

The lights go out for good. Too much time has passed before you realize it's not just another rolling blackout. The time to bug-out safely has passed. Group members are scattered all over the city, with several key members out-of-town, unable to make it back to meet up with you. Stress and panic prevail as 2000 lbs. of equipment fail to fit into an ill-conceived bug-out vehicle and trailer because a pre-positioned destination and supplies were not determined in advance. One member breaks down and decides to ride it out in their basement. Your own children tell you you're crazy and sit in the front yard without budging, in defiance because you won't pack the PlayStation 4.

Fear turns into anger and then into rage. The next morning, travelling eastward towards no-man's-land, your vehicle runs out of fuel on a lonely, back-country road, while trying to circumvent the next chaotic metropolitan area. After abandoning your vehicle and walking for three days, you come upon a hastily constructed checkpoint, which appears a hundred meters past the turn in the road. Unfortunately, the checkpoint was created by a ruthless street gang and your demise is all but sealed. This is the REAL ending.

The Bug-Out Plan

Here is an easy acronym to use to ensure you're never the "LAST OUT."

L ocation

A lternative Routes

S upplies

T iming

O bservation

U niformity

T ransportation

Location

Being able to locate and communicate with family or group members will be of major importance. The dream is that everyone is in the same location and ready to go when the balloon goes up. Reality usually dictates otherwise. It's always best to assume that the family or group will be scattered across the city at best, and at worst, out-of-town, with limited or no means of communication. These factors complicate and unravel any good bug-out plan. Even the most decorated combat veteran will feel the gut-wrenching pain when he realizes that loved ones are unreachable. Communication or a complete understanding of when and where to meet will be required to keep order. Therefore, I recommend purchasing hand-held, HAM radios for each member of your family/group, as well as have pre-determined meeting locations.

Alternative Routes
It's critical that two distinct routes be mapped out, with different rally points, on the way to your final destination. A rally point is a place designated by the leader, where the group moves to reassemble and reorganize if it becomes dispersed. Rally points must be easy to find, have cover and concealment, be away from natural lines of drift, and be defendable for short periods.

The first route will be for an early bug-out, when the timing is perfect and all roads are still open, as mass panic will not have yet ensued. This itinerary will allow you the freedom to travel at will, through small cities and towns, however, it is still advisable that you avoid major metropolitan areas.

The second route will detail how not only to avoid all major metropolitan areas, but how to also circumvent smaller cities and towns, especially those with bridges (and tunnels) that cross key terrain (water, mountains, and gorges). No matter where you live or what your intended route is, there will ALWAYS be at least one bridge to contend with, that is why you need to find at least one alternate route without one. You might as well consider bridges to be brick walls instead. If the bridge is taken over by friend or foe, and you are turned away or ambushed, all bets are off. Do you have your route planned to cross over key terrain features well outside of town? Have you driven your route at least once, all the way to your retreat? A dry run would be in good order; even if you have to use all of your vacation time in doing so, and have to drag your dogs and kids around, you will at least have a fighting chance if the time ever comes when your plan turns into a reality. If you think that you can just pick the route as you go… well… then… all I can say is good luck.

The best advice is to have pre-planned rally points and schedules vacuum-sealed in water-tight packets that are packed in every vehicle owned, as well as stored in whatever survival bags that are prepared. Each member of the team/family should have their own copies in the above locations as well. It's much easier to just open and read instructions during stressful events that were previously well-thought-out and arranged, rather than make-up plans as you go along. Your plans should include locations of cached supplies, rally points, meeting times, and step-by-step, color-coded flow charts directing certain actions.

These plans may be in a constant state of flux, as members will travel out-of-town for work or go on vacation. They should be updated to fit the itineraries of those that travel far and wide. For instance, for out-of-town members, rally points may be impractical, thus, the main objective for them would solely be to arrive to the final destination safely. In this event, this will turn into a waiting game, as there will be no way to know how quickly they will be able to make it to the pre-designated retreat, if ever (depending on the severity of the crisis and the distance they are from the meeting location).

Supplies
Your supplies will both hinder your movement, as well as provide you with the means to keep on moving. Always pack your bug-out bag with the option for dismounted travel. Remember, these packs are built light to allow you to move RAPIDLY towards your rally points and then to your final destination, where hopefully all of your preps are awaiting you.

Your own needs will dictate how light or how heavy and burdensome this pack will be in the end. The YouTube "myths" will tell you that you can carry an 80-lb. pack and an M1a rifle, with a full-battle load, as you travel all the way from Florida to your hidden retreat in Montana. But the truth of the matter says you're better off with a 25-lb. pack and a handgun. You decide; either way, you will likely end up walking to your retreat in almost any scenario, so tread lightly, VERY lightly. Water is heavy, but the purification equipment is much lighter, so carry less water between rally points and fill up when you're unsure of the lay of the land. Topographical maps of your entire route will allow you to plan for water recovery breaks (consider the seasonality of water availability), which will allow for less of a load.

Timing
Timing, as they say, is EVERYTHING. Timing will dictate who arrives to leave with you, the routes that you will be able to take, and of course, if you will be able to leave at all. The key to getting out alive is to leave before full public knowledge has hit, for when this occurs, pandemonium will

ensue. How many people watched as the Towers fell on 9-11, only a few blocks away, and ultimately died because they were too close to the destruction and were hit by debris? How many more will perish in the next local, regional, or national disaster by watching the events unfold, frozen in shock, unable to move? Remember, it's better to be a few minutes, hours, or even years too early, than a second too late!

Do you live in Maryland and own a retreat in Montana? Congratulations! You had better leave early or be a pilot, because time will not be on your side. Storing up sick and vacation days that can be used at the last minute will give you the opportunity to flee when the handwriting is on the wall, rather than quitting a job too early, just to find out that your worries didn't really materialize. In this way, you are in a win-win situation. First, it's not only great training, but dry runs always pay off later. One day, you will be ahead of the stagnate freeways filled with zombies. One never actually knows how it will all play out, but that's half the fun of being a prepper.

Observation and Intel
In conjunction with timing is observing your surroundings and intelligence gathering. It can be difficult to keep the big picture in mind as the world appears to be crumbling before one's very eyes. Step away from the here and now and relax; take a moment to "see" the world around you. Assessing everything from traffic flow to the actions of people on the streets will help determine if this is "the event" that requires activation and implementation of the bug-out plan. Accurate intelligence from any inside sources working in various sectors of our society will be invaluable. Are any of your group members' law enforcement officers, firefighters/paramedics, ER doctors, on active duty, in the financial business, or in any other jobs that may be privy to inside information as threats unfold? Are any people that you trust quietly packing up and leaving?

Arrogance in regard to your network, your group, and your plans can lead one to miss finite details that would otherwise warn of impending doom. Remember, you're not as good as you think you are. As you move along your evacuation route, obtaining intel will be key, so try and converse with anyone that may look like they have information, if it's safe to do so, of course.

What's to be learned here: Fast and accurate situational observation/awareness and intelligence gathering is the key to activating the evacuation plan and bugging-out before the masses realize what's going on. The sooner one leaves, the farther the final destination can ultimately be. Again, the sooner one leaves, the farther the final destination can be. If only one fact from this chapter is remembered, let it be that.

Uniformity of Preps

Getting two or more preppers to agree on a "group standard system of preps," as coined by James Wesley Rawles, in his first book, Patriots: Surviving the Coming Collapse, is like asking to US to partner with Cuba. It's sad that this has to be mentioned, but the reality is that this lack of uniformity will lead to the undoing of many small prepper groups during peaceful times and the death of many more during tumultuous times.

The best advice that I can give to any small group of preppers is for each and every individual in the group to swallow their pride by agreeing on a "group standard system of preps" that all members will store and use. This system should always include such things as water-purification equipment, fire starters, medical kits, communi-cations gear, energy-creation equipment, and finally, of course, defensive tools. Essentially, what this means is that each member will store EXACTLY the same items as the other members, down to the make and model. Why is this necessary, you might ask? Well, imagine you are in a fire fight and you run out of ammo and you ask the guy right next to you for another magazine; do you think it would be problematic if he hands you an AK-47 mag for your AR-15 rifle? Use this same example for any number of things, from flashlights that use the same batteries to matching topographical maps that are already marked. You get the point.

Transportation

As you probably remember, the "LAST OUT" acronym ends with "transportation," which we will thoroughly cover in the next chapter. However, I would like to take this opportunity to discuss dismounted travel on foot instead.

For those of you out there that are not in shape, the word "dismounted travel" should scare the hell out of you. No more fantasy, survival-novel-dream scenarios about walking from Miami to Montana. It's time for a reality check. If you can't grab your bug-out bag, along with rifle and vest, while running out the door to complete the following, then you will likely not stand a chance.

- 5-mile walk with 100-yard sprints in between each mile

- 100 sit-ups

- 10 pull-ups

- 25 push-ups

This is not a Special Forces/Special Operations fitness test; it is a wake-up call. Stop buying cases of ammo and new guns; save your cash and buy a treadmill instead. Ask yourself if you could defend your family AFTER a massive physical endeavor such as the one above, while adding the psychological impact of a societal collapse on top of that. If you've never been in combat, go find someone that has. You'll be surprised at what they tell you. Whatever it takes, get in shape; the success of your bug-out plan depends on it!

One last bit of advice: Keep paper maps on hand, as GPS units and other navigational gear may be unserviceable in a grid-down scenario. Always have a back-up plan to any sort of technology during a bug-out.

13
LAND, AIR, AND SEA BUG-OUT

You no doubt have seen the news stories of masses of people trying to evacuate ahead of a hurricane or impending disaster. The roads are full and along them are the vehicles that had some kind of trouble and are now stalled. You don't want to be that poor soul stuck on the side of the road, in the middle of an evacuation route waiting for help.

In this chapter we will review different types of bug-out vehicles (BOV), what you need to know about each one, and why you need to have one.

When considering what BOV is right for you, you will first have to assess for the five pillars of protection and preparedness: reliability, sustainability, durability, versatility, and payload capacity. In addition, you will have to determine what your price range will be.

What does a bug-out motor vehicle need?

- First and foremost, your BOV should be a 4 x 4, with upgraded shocks/springs. This will make your escape through rural country a tad bit easier and will allow you to haul more stuff.
- Some beefy tires or mudders would work the best for off-road use. Don't forget to carry a spare tire in case of a blowout.

- Your BOV should have a front/rear hitch and a front/rear wench for towing and for pulling yourself out of sticky situations, e.g., the hole was deeper than you thought it was.
- Your BOV should be in good working condition and tested often, i.e., driven every weekend to make sure everything is still in working order.
- Your BOV should include skid plates, brush guards, fog lights, gas-tank protection, and a quality CB with a spring-based whip antenna.
- Make sure that your BOV has an upgraded fan shroud, in order to prevent the engine from stalling due to water spray, while providing more power, which is very important when hauling heavy loads.

Types of Bug-Out Vehicles (BOVs)

We surely are living in a marvelous time, where technology is making some really amazing advances in the survival and preparedness field— albeit expensive technology, but amazing nonetheless. The type of BOV you choose will solely depend on your preferences and your individual situation. With this in mind, consider all of the options that are available to you.

The 1970's BOV
The classic BOV, and the most preferred by preppers on a budget, is the old, but reliable, 1970's pickup or SUV, equipped with a 4×4 drive. The reason the prepper community has flocked to these BOV models is more for their lack of

electronic components, than out of an attempt to be thrifty. The assumption out there is that older BOVs are "somewhat" less susceptible to EMPs (electromagnetic pulses), which are caused by solar flares and nuclear blasts. Unfortunately, this is just a theory, as there is no evidence to that effect.

Another good reason to own an older vehicle is because there are less electronics to be tampered with: no GPS tracking (i.e., Onstar), less things to go wrong, and easier to fix (with a basic understanding of automotive mechanics). Additionally, these BOVs are much more cost effective than their newer counterparts. Mileage, however, will be a big issue, so let's pray that there won't be a fuel shortage.

Military-Grade BOV
On average, a military BOVs' starting cost will be $10,000. Of course, the price can go up substantially depending on what model you decide to choose. Military BOVs can be purchased through

Craigslist or eBay. The best feature military vehicles have is their fuel versatility. They can use any flammable fluid; it will certainly cause buildup, but at least it'll run.

Military-grade BOVs, like the HMMWV (high-mobility multipurpose wheeled vehicle), have an independent suspension system with a 4×4 drive set-up. Their raised driveshaft trains allow for a lower center-of-gravity and their run flat tires ensure that they are puncture-proof. What's the downside? Well, without proper maintenance, you'd better be well informed on HMMWV mechanics or bring a Marine along for the ride.

Motorcycle BOV
One very popular, recurring theme is bugging-out on a motorcycle. This may seem like a great idea on the surface due to its maneuverability and excellent fuel economy, but safety is of first and foremost importance.

Here are a few reasons why bugging-out on a motorcycle is a bad idea.

While a motorcycle's fuel economy beats a car, truck, or SUV, it has only a fraction of their fuel capacity, so all-in-all, a motorcycle will have about the same range-of-distance that the others will. Bugging-out on a motorcycle means taking very little gear and supplies, and at most, two passengers. A motorcycle provides no protection from the elements or from attackers. A snow storm or a kid with a rock can end your life while riding on a motorcycle. If you happen to fall or crash, you face far more serious injuries than if you were in an automobile—without EMS, this is more likely to be fatal. Also, long-distance travel on a motorcycle can take a toll on your body.

On the other hand, a motorcycle can be a good choice if you are bugging-out alone to a known location that is already stocked with food and supplies and is relatively close by.

Before bugging-out on a motorcycle, it's important to carefully weigh all variables, including:

- What terrain must you cross in order to reach your bug-out location?
- How far must you travel?
- What will the traffic and weather conditions be like?
- What is the threat level? (Are you bugging-out to avoid a hurricane or civil unrest?)
- How many people will be traveling with you?
- What kind of gear and supplies will you be bringing?

Your Everyday Driver
To be honest, I think this is where many of us are at. Those who can't afford a $10,000, retrofitted, military-grade BOV will have to rely upon their daily driver. For instance, this could be your 2001 Jeep Grand Cherokee 4 x 4 that your family uses for day-to-day activities.

The first benefit is no additional costs to your family. Rather than buying a separate BOV, discrete modifications can be made in order to make it a go-between for getting the kids to school and for fleeing from school if the need arises. In this instance, it is unlikely that you will be able to keep this thing fully stocked and ready to rock. Since day-to-day life comes first, making room for Jimmy's soccer balls and little Maggie's pompoms is of first priority, but to remedy this, just keep your bug-out gear stocked and at the ready so that non-essentials and essentials can be switched-out at a moment's notice.

Make a game out of bugging-out. There is no need to freak the kids out. Just make it a fun little exercise, with the goal of having your bug-out vehicle packed and ready to depart in 5 minutes flat.

Prepare Your BOV
Now that you've determined what BOV will work for you, it's time to stock it. I will list a few helpful items that should have a place in your vehicle survival bag or container.

- Repair manual for your vehicle
- Mechanics toolset that includes metric/standard sockets and wrenches
- Ball-peen hammer
- Locking pliers and channel-lock pliers
- Lineman's pliers
- Needle-nose pliers
- Torque and standard wrench sets
- Fuses and bulbs
- Vehicle fluids (oil, coolant, brake fluid, transmission fluid, and distilled water)
- Electrical and duct tape

- WD-40
- LED Flashlight with extra batteries
- Breaker bar
- RTV sealant
- Starter fluid
- Degreaser
- Fix-A-Flat
- Jack
- Jumper cables
- Rope
- Tow straps
- 5-10 gallons of extra fuel
- Tarp
- Work gloves
- First-aid kit
- Hard copy maps
- Heavy-duty rope
- Baby wipes
- Blankets
- Collapsible shovel
- Extra tire

Bicycle BOV

In a long-term, post SHTF world, there won't be sufficient motor-vehicle supplies (gas, oil, tires, and repair parts); therefore, a bike will become a primary means of movement for most of us. My suggestion is that your bug-out plan makes provisions for a bicycle.

The Rationale

- Cycling is less energy intensive than walking and can help one reach their destination much faster than on foot.
- Bicycles are everywhere and so are their parts.
- They are simple to maintain and ride.

- Tools are available at a low cost.
- 20 miles or more can be covered easily.
- A bike can be picked-up and carried over short distances.
- Bikes can be used as scout vehicles.
- A bike is stealthy. You can move quickly, but without the noise made by a motor vehicle.
- It has no license plate by which you can be identified.
- You can customize your bike according to your requirements. (A flat, camouflage paint job will make it practically invisible!)
- You can add a compact trailer to the back of your bike in order to carry your survival kit.
- Even if you don't ride it, it can be used to carry your gear.

My Requirements for a Bug-Out Bike

- It should be suitable for daily use so that it is ridden often, otherwise, you will not be aware of maintenance issues until it is too late.
- Your bike should be suitable for going on-road and off-road, with thorn-resistant tubes.
- It should be comfortable to ride.
- It should fit your body size and weight properly.
- Your bike should have a sturdy frame that is also lightweight.
- Don't buy a fancy bike that requires special tools to repair; it needs to be easy to fix during a disaster scenario.
- It should be able to fit inside a vehicle or be mounted on to the outside.
- Consider a set-up that allows for front and rear mounting of your gear.
- Don't buy an expensive bike that will be vulnerable to theft.

Before putting together a bug-out bicycle, it's important to carefully weigh all variables, like the ones listed for the motorcycle. As you are probably well aware, a bicycle will provide no protection from the elements or from attackers.

Kamp-Rite's Midget Bushtrekka
If you're heading out on a long-distance, lone-wolf bug-out, you'll need to bring along sleeping accommodations. But why squeeze into an awkward, one-person tent when you can haul your own miniature, pop-up camper?

Kamp-Rite's Midget Bushtrekka not only trans-
forms into a luxurious tent and cot that keeps you
off the ground when sleeping, but it also has over
41 gallons of storage space, so don't worry, there
is no need to load-up your bike with saddle bags.
Its four wheels all operate independently, so it can
handle most bumpy terrain, but you're probably
going to want to avoid extreme mountain trails
with this in tow.

If your bike has a catastrophic failure, you will still
have the means of carrying your bug-out gear by
"MacGyvering-it" into a rickshaw. I have gone on
countless hikes with my wife and kids and must
embarrassingly admit that I have my wife carry our
baby, and I wear my day pack, while everyone's
water and snacks get pushed around in the baby's
stroller—how I love the invention of the wheel!

As a matter of fact, I have a friend in the USMC
who has stated that the armed forces, in general,

are looking into what looks like a Deer Cart Game
Hauler for carrying their ridiculously heavy ruck
packs and field gear. Imagine how many back
injuries would be prevented and how much less
fatigue the soldiers would face if this sort of thing
was implemented in the field.

Dixon Rollerpack

I have thought about getting the Dixon Rollerpack, since I kind of like the bug-out, stroller setup. The manufacturer states that it will roll over logs and large rocks, maneuver between trees, go up and down hills, and turn with ease. You will have to sidestep a bit to get it around a tight turn, and when you stop, you will have to back-it-in, like you are backing a car into a parking spot. The Dixon Rollerpack also has a hip belt that can be used, so that it can be worn as a pack when folded up.

Boats

Some people will immediately dismiss the idea of using a boat as a means to bug-out. In researching the concept for this book, I went to all of the popular blogs and forums, reading-up on everything that I could find. It didn't take very long, as there wasn't much out there. At first, that seemed like good news, because I like to write about things that no one else has. However, what little I did find on the web basically dismissed the idea due to impracticality.

Now, I can list a dozen reasons why a boat isn't the best choice for a BOV, but practicality isn't one of them. I then asked myself, "What am I missing here?"

I believe most people initially think of boats as exclusive to the ultra-wealthy. That's not entirely accurate. You can purchase one in reasonable condition for about the same price as a trailer camper these days. Now, I'm not talking about a yacht, but something like a mid-sized sailboat. I see ads for hundreds of 25-35 ft. vessels for less than $50,000. There are numerous tax advantages for buying a boat and many banks offer financing similar to that of a home mortgage.

Now, low-end, used boats are known to be a money pit. Boats are similar to campers in that stuff breaks on them all the time. But as a BOV, they don't have to be fully functional and ready for a transatlantic voyage. When you compare a boat to a piece of country property, complete with shelter, water and food supply, a boat starts looking like a bargain from a financial perspective.

Many boats are designed to be self-sufficient for long periods of time. This statement should cause the average prepper to perk up and pay attention. Many vessels have desalinators, or water makers, for a virtually unlimited supply of fresh water. They have sewage systems, redundant power systems, and huge fuel-storage capacities. All of these are normally high on anyone's list of preps. A 35-ft., used sail boat that I recently looked at was designed for four adults to enjoy for extended stays onboard. It was $29,000. It had solar power, a generator, a 12-volt to 115 AC inverter, a full kitchen, two showers, a microwave, two televisions, a radar, GPS, VHF radio, a dual-voltage frig, a dual-voltage freezer, an ice maker, and a water maker. Its little diesel motor could move it along at about 10 mi/gal without using the sails at all. Its 80-gal fuel tank could run the generator for quite a long time.

If you want to discuss food supplies, it would be difficult to debate anything being better than having a boat, as anywhere you travel, fish, kelp and costal plants should be easy to come by. Throw in a well-thought-out "deck garden," and you practically have an infinite food supply.

On a boat, electrical energy is a mixed bag. Many sailing vessels have wind turbines and solar systems with limited power. Huge banks of batteries are not uncommon. Some modern vessels even have electric drives. Almost every vessel over 28-ft. has a generator. If it isn't already, it wouldn't be that hard to make a boat independent of the grid.

From a security standpoint, a boat would get mixed reviews. It would be difficult to imagine being able to isolate one's self more than by being on a boat. The only security exposure from being water bound would be trouble with concealment. Depending on your geographic location, that may or may not be a problem. Along many islands and coasts are private coves where one could hide for a period of time, then move along as the need arises.

A boat makes sense for a BOV in all of the major categories we prep for. On a boat, food, shelter, energy, water, and security are all equal to, or perhaps better than, their landlocked alternatives. What strikes me is their ability to have a dual usage. Boating is also fun for the whole family. Even if it never leaves the marina, being on or around the water can be a recreational delight.

Flying to Your Retreat

One of the biggest challenges we must face is how we would manage to get from our normal residences to our retreats if and when a major disaster is about to occur (or has already occurred).

The ideal choice is, of course, to simply hop into the family car and drive to the prepared destination. Doing this, however, would only be possible if you were able to anticipate any such disaster, otherwise, the roads would become clogged and turn into a giant parking lot once others decided to do the same thing as you did.

Let's explore the usefulness of planes for not only avoiding road congestion, but for other reasons as well.

A plane can, of course, get you anywhere quicker than any motor vehicle can.

Ariel recon is certainly an added bonus.

A plane can allow you to delay your decision to bug-out, because you don't need to be so con-cerned about beating the traffic.

A plane gives you an alternate method to get you to where you're going. Maybe the roads are closed due to bad weather or as a side effect of the situation that triggered the crisis. An earthquake, for example, might have caused bridges to fall or an erupting volcano might destroy roads with molten lava runs.

Weather issues may have a much greater impact on travel by road than by air. For instance, if a road is washed out, it may not be able to be repaired again. If a heavy snowfall occurs, there may be no snow removal crews and no snow removal equipment to clear the road, causing it to remain closed all winter long.

While planes are also weather dependent to an extent, the type of weather issues that affect them are short-term rather than long-term.

Most single-engine planes don't have more range than a car that is well stocked with fuel would, but their speed means that what might be a two or three day journey by car would be a comfortable, single day journey or less in a plane, with just one take-off and one landing.

Since plane travel is not dependent on roads, you can essentially travel anywhere, as long as there is an airstrip/runway, whereas the roads underneath you might meander around and detour through dog-leg loops, adding hundreds of miles to your journey. In this way flying will take you to your destination directly, just "as a crow flies," and within the shortest amount of time too.

Plane travel is also safer—no worries of being carjacked, hassled by law enforcement, or being stuck with the hoards due to a road block.

Since we have listed all of the pros, we should also consider the cons. Cost may be prohibitive and one must consider storage. Do you live next to a general aviation airport that can store a private plane and where planes can fly in and out of?

There are also limitations in terms of how many people and how much cargo can be carried, assuming you get a small, single-engine plane. The only way around this, though, may be to ferry people and materials to your retreat in two or three trips, assuming that you have enough fuel and time on your side.

Seaplanes

Maybe your normal residence or your retreat is closer to a lake or sheltered bay than to an airport. In such cases, a seaplane is better than a regular plane, in the sense that it has the capability of taking off from water or from land. On that note, airports can experience the same problems that roadways can, i.e., an earthquake can rip up a runway just as easily as a roadway, so a seaplane has a most definite advantage. In a crisis, a regular plane would have to operate under emergency air-traffic-control restrictions, which would impede private flying. However, landing on water would eliminate such limitations.

Imagine having the extra advantage of a boat with you in the form of your seaplane. Envision landing at your remote lake, dropping anchor, and casting for a lunker trout, bass, or pike.

The word "seaplane" is used to describe two types of air/water vehicles: the floatplane and the flying boat. A float plane is one particular type of sea plane. Just like the sea plane, it can take off from land as well as from a water surface. These planes are attached with special types of floats or pontoons; this is why they are also called pontoon planes. These extra fittings allow them to float on water. A float plane, however, is more weather dependent than a flying boat.

Flying boats are planes that use pontoons attached to the fuselage to enable them to float on water. The use of a huge hull provides buoyant force to float on water against gravity. The use of hull provides huge surface area, with the added advantage of being able to handle severe weather conditions such as high waves and tides during take-off and landing. The disadvantage is that as the name, flying boat, implies, there is no use for it on land.

Whether a float plane or a flying boat, all sea-planes are only capable of flying during daylight hours, which is why your flight hours will vary depending on the season you find yourself in.

Helicopters

Helicopters are unique in that they can get in and out of places where all other aircraft cannot. They can take off and land in very compact areas. This is why most rescue operations and special-ops teams use helicopters exclusively. Maneuverability in the air is also unparalleled. They can travel between tall buildings and through forests and mountains. If weather permits, I cannot think of a faster and more direct way out of a crowded city than by helicopter. Helicopters can deliver people and goods to extremely remote bug-out locations that may not be accessible by any other vehicle or even by foot. The downside, however, is that a lot of training is required in order to operate one and a big bank account is needed in order to buy one.

14
THE IDEAL RETREAT

Deciding exactly where to relocate is not an exact science. You can gauge potential threats and plan accordingly, but you can never be completely certain what will happen and where the safest place will be. However, knowing that you have researched and prepared the best retreat possible puts you at a far greater advantage, by allowing you to stock more supplies and be more prepared for long-term emergencies.

There is an apocryphal story about a man who was living in Virginia in the late 1850s. He could see the U.S. Civil War brewing, and he wanted no part of it. He realized that his native Virginia was likely to be heavily contested territory, so he set about finding the safest place possible where he could shelter his family during the coming war. After much searching and deliberation he finally found a peaceful place that was far, far away from where the anticipated battles would occur. He moved his family up to Pennsylvania, to a little farming town that you may have heard of—Gettysburg.

As you can see, there are no perfect locations, but there are certainly places that will, for the most part, be better than others.

Location and land characteristics are crucial factors when a person is considering purchasing land for a survival retreat. A survival retreat should be a well-prepared and defensible stronghold.

As evidenced by Hurricane Katrina in 2005, population density is perhaps the most crucial factor to consider when selecting a safe haven. If a major disaster occurs, living in a more isolated area (especially from major highways) will help to protect you from transient mobs leaving the cities. You don't want your retreat to be near main routes that are connected to major cities, as towns along these roads will be hit hard by hordes of people. The big cities on the Gulf Coast became hell holes, whereas the small towns were able to get by fairly well. Anywhere east of the Missouri River has too much population! The Northeast is also downwind from some major nuclear targets. Although many believe that living in the warm climates of the South will be an ideal area for retreats, keep in mind that most Southern states are susceptible to damage brought on by hurricanes, tropical storms, and flooding.

It is recommended that you select a retreat in a mixed farming/ranching/timber region, in a low-humidity area. Living in coastal regions is of concern due to the risk of tidal waves or hurricanes, oil-tanker mishaps, visits by foreign terrorists, and because of the outside chance of dramatically rising or falling sea levels in the event of a climate shift. Beware of anywhere within 150 miles of the Mexican border, as the crime rate is higher near the border, and there could be a huge influx of illegal immigrants in an apocalyptic scenario.

Once you have selected a potential region to concentrate on, select an experienced local real-estate agent. Odds are that you won't be able to find one that specializes in retreat properties, so it may take a while and a few false starts before your agent begins showing you the right type of locations. While walking around the property, note what resources and obstacles the site has before making a potential plan. Keep in mind that you want to find a property that can be sustainable. The following is a basic criteria list that you can give a real-estate agent. (Tailor to suit your particular needs):

What to Look for in a Bug-Out Property

- Property that backs up to a state or national park
- A fair amount of timber
- Semi-isolated location: low population density and away from major cities and suburban developments
- Not in the path of real estate developers.

- Steady, natural water supply: sufficient year-round precipitation, surface water, and/or a spring fed or artesian well. (Pumped well water would be an inferior second choice.)
- Southern exposure—particularly important at higher elevations
- Rich topsoil
- Minimal noxious weeds, i.e., Russian thistle, teasel, Russian knapweed, yellow star thistle, etc.
- Sunny area for solar panels
- No major earthquake, hurricane, or tornado risks
- Not on a flood plain
- No tidal-wave risk (at least two-hundred ft. above sea level)
- Minimal forest-fire risk
- Away from interstate freeways and other channelized areas **OR** panoramic views: Decide on one or the other, but don't buy a property that has neither attribute.
- A diverse and healthy local economy
- Low-housing costs.
- Low taxes
- Non-intrusive scale of local/state government—what kind of laws are in place?
- Favorable zoning and inexpensive building permits
- If it has an existing house, a house with fireproof/ballistically-protected-masonry construction. Note: If it is also in an earthquake-prone area, you might weigh the odds in this regard and opt instead for more earthquake-safe, timber-frame construction.
- Minimal gun laws

- A location geared toward a lifestyle of self-sufficiency
- Plentiful, local sources of wood or coal
- No restrictions on keeping livestock
- Not near a prison or large mental-health institution
- Inexpensive insurance rates (home, auto, and health)
- Upwind and away from major nuclear-power plants
- An active, growing farmer's market

Items of Interest to Study and Questions to Ask Yourself

- Compare counties that you are interested in moving to.
- Research websites like www.city-data.com to see what the statistics are for the location you are considering.
- Consider the relative grid-power independence and stability of various regions by referencing www.npr.org: "Visualizing The U.S. Electric Grid" in the search bar.
- Visit http://msc.fema.gov/portal/ to determine flood risk.
- Take a long hard look at the "City Lights of the United States" at http://earthobservatory.nasa.gov. NASA scientists use city light data to map urbanization. A picture tells a thousand words.

- Go to www.nytimes.com and search for "Where to Live to Avoid a Natural Disaster"
- Navigate droughtmonitor.unl.edu to determine regional drought in the U.S.

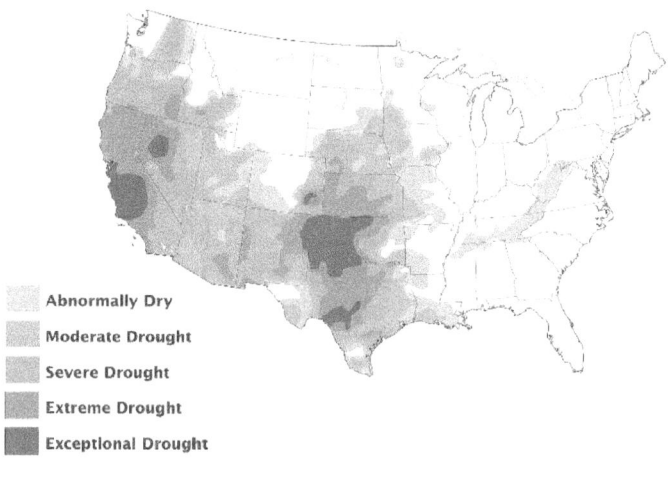

Abnormally Dry
Moderate Drought
Severe Drought
Extreme Drought
Exceptional Drought

- Use a mapping tool to locate underground aquifers in the area.
- Study topographic and geographic maps of the area.
- Find a prepper-friendly church: seek sound doctrine, not "programs".
- Map the vegetation growth in the area.
- If it suits your fancy, research home schooling laws and home birth laws.
- What type of employment is in the area?
- Can you work with or learn to work with the available materials?
- What can be used at the site—trees, bamboo, stones, sand, soil, clay…?
- Can you protect your land if attacked? Do you have defensible terrain?
- Can the retreat property be seen from the road?
- Are there any environmental or climate issues to consider?
- Is there a long growing season? Reference The Old Farmer's Almanac at www.almanac.com to find out.
- Is this an active farming community with an abundance of livestock and produce that are readily available?
- Is there an already active barter system in place?

Keeping these considerations and questions in mind will help you to determine whether the property is appropriate for surviving long-term disasters.

15
APARTMENT PREPPING

According to the National Multi-Housing Council, about 34% of the US population lives in apartments. That's 40,119,000 renters. If we were to include condo owners, the stat would be at least twice as large. The point here is that there are quite a few preppers who share limited space with other individuals. Apartment residents have special considerations to keep in mind while stockpiling for uncertain times. Less space than a traditional home offers and reduced privacy are two of the main reasons for this. Fear not, for there are still ways to implement an effective prepping strategy.

Maximizing Potential Storage Space
Living in an apartment clearly does not give you the sustainable space for gear and other storage that a house does, depending of course on the size of the house. Space is limited, and an apartment dweller may feel like a hoarder or a junk dealer.

Fortunately, space planners have devised a multitude of tricks to get more use out of small spaces. If you're looking to maximize your storage options, here are some tips to consider.

In the Bedroom

Store clothes under your bed. Most home stores sell plastic-storage boxes of various heights that you can use to take advantage of space between the floor and your box spring assuming that you don't sleep on a futon.

Consider a platform bed with built-in drawers. Some manufacturers even make bed platforms already equipped with pull-out drawers. These are sometimes referred to as a "captain's bed" or "mate's bed." This negates the need to buy additional storage boxes.

Don't forget the headboard. Look for a headboard with built-in shelves or hidden storage cubbies.

Turn a closet into a storage facility. Equip a spare closet, or even your main closet, with shelves and hang a floating clothes rack near an empty wall. Place a shoe rack against another empty wall as well. In this way, your closet can be used for your survival supplies, instead of for your clothes and shoes.

In the Living Room

Get a chest that doubles as a coffee table. That flat surface in front of your sofa contains plenty of airspace between the floor and tabletop. Find a nice, low-profile chest, preferably one with pull-out drawers, and use in place of a conventional coffee table.

Use storage ottomans as bar stools. Line three or four, tall storage ottomans in front of your breakfast bar. In this way you will have more places to store your stuff, plus a place for you and others to sit.

Go deep. With some ingenuity and drawer runners, you can equip a deep bookshelf with pullout drawers that will allow you to maximize the entire shelf space.

In the Kitchen

Hang Your Pots and Pans. Maximize your precious kitchen space by suspending pots and pans from ceiling hangers. This will not only free up under-cabinet storage, but make you look like a serious cook as well!

Dining Room

Use the floor beneath your dining table for a storage space, and then cover the table to overflowing with a large enough table cloth to hide the contents within.

In the Bathroom

Install narrow shelves, racks, or ledges. Strategically placed wall-mounted shelves, racks, or ledges can increase storage area in even the smallest spaces.

Install recessed shelving in bathroom "nooks." Some bathrooms have wasted nooks and crannies that can be made useful by installing recessed-and-ready shelving.

In any Room

When in doubt, look up. Take full advantage of all the vertical volume your living space has to offer. Fill what areas you can with stock cabinets or other pre-made storage units. Another option would be to purchase an overhead storage rack.

Beyond your Apartment

Consider renting a storage unit within walking distance.

Storage units can be found in nearly every city or town across the country, even in most small towns. Renting a storage facility in a town near your bug-out location allows for a few things. You get to learn the lay of the land you will have to travel; you will also have a secure place for all of your supplies. "Secure" may be an overstatement, however, as anyone can come along with bolt cutters and cut the lock off, unless you purchase a discus padlock, that is.

The Brinks discus padlock is quite affordable and can be found for $10-$15 each or in packs of two for a little over $20. It obviously isn't the cheapest padlock around, but with a steel shackle that is thick and very resistant to prying, cutting, and sawing, it's hard to find a better padlock that will keep your belongings secure.

Ascertaining a storage unit also gives you a backup plan in case you are gone from your apartment and you can't get back to it during a crisis. The same would apply in the event that your apartment becomes damaged or destroyed—you would have extra, accessible supplies. Just remember to be careful with food storage in these units due to extreme temperature variability.

Security

If you are allowed, get and install a monitored wireless alarm system. Homes and apartments with security systems displaying the window stickers that the home is alarmed are three times less likely to be broken into than those that do not have them. That is a real-life statistic.

You may have to provide the landlord with a code for access to your apartment. The alarm system may not have to have heat or fire detection, as you already should have that in your apartment per the building code.

If you live on the first floor of an apartment building or home with an apartment in it, it becomes even more important, because your apartment is that much more accessible than a second- or third-floor apartment.

Privacy

Yes, it's already a given that if you live in an apartment, you share your walls, ceiling, and floors with total strangers, but what's more concerning is the fact that you are not the only one with a key to your apartment. While it is expected that the management office should contact you in case someone has to enter your place, this is not always the case. Maintenance workers are the most common individuals that might have to gain access to your apartment, and the last thing you want is for them to see everything that you have. It is prudent, therefore, to keep your supplies hidden, covered, or out-of-sight, if possible.

Have a Water Plan

Space in your apartment will be limited, so it is doubtful that you will be storing a 275 gal. tote of water, but consider storing stackable water any-where there is some floor space. A good choice would be the Legacy Premium, 5-gal. water box. With thick, tough-to-puncture, BPA-free plastic bags protected by heavy-duty cardboard boxes, storing water has never been simpler. Another option is purchasing the boxed, 1-gal. jugs of bottled water—six, 1-gal. jugs per box. These boxes are easily stackable. If they aren't visible at your local grocer, just ask one of the attendants if some can be brought to you from the back.

Many preppers are very familiar with the big, 55-gal. blue water barrels. While effective for storing great amounts of water, those containers are impossible to move, waste space, and lack a spigot for quick access to water. Legacy Premium 5-gal. containers stack perfectly on top of each other to maximize storage, are easy to fill, with a filling hose compatible with any faucet, weigh 40 lbs once full, have a built-in spigot for quick, easy water access, and include Aquamira water treatment drops, which will make your water potable for 5 years. If no emergency occurs within 5 years, just empty the container, fill it up again, and treat for another 5 years of storage. Heavy-duty cardboard containers also keep sunlight from penetrating the water pouch, extending the shelf life of the water and the pouch as well. Unfortunately, these water boxes do not come cheap, however.

In addition, you can also look into items like the Water Bob, which can be utilized to store 60 gal. of water in your tub for drinking/sanitation purposes. No matter how much water you have stored, you will eventually need to find local sources of fresh water and have a way to get some of that water back to your apartment for filtering. Pick up a good water filter, like the Berkey, and get familiar with using it.

Never underestimate the importance of water. If the power goes out and the taps run dry, you will see people going crazy while looking for fresh water.

Food Storage
Making sure that you use your space efficiently is very important when storing the maximum amount of food in the smallest amount of space. This can be very difficult to do, that is why food buckets are so convenient and are such a space saver--they are stackable and easy to move around.

If you are blessed enough to have storage space in the basement of your apartment building, please make sure that anything you store down there is sealed well, several times over, especially in metal and plastic, airtight containers, to keep the creepy-crawly vermin out of it. You will also want to camouflage anything that is not in plastic or metal containers in order to keep others in your apartment building unaware of your preps.

Another option that you might consider is using a friend or family member's home, that lives close by, assuming that they are of the same mind set and don't mind, of course.

Growing a Small Garden
If you have the space on your deck, terrace, or balcony, consider growing a small garden. This will help augment your food supplies, as well as get you used to nurturing the kind of plants that will be feeding you in the future, at your bug-out location, for instance.

Have A Good Exit Strategy

Unfortunately, there are real downsides to apartments and apartment buildings that there is just no way of getting around. No matter how secure they may be, you are still in the semipublic eye due to all of the other inhabitants living there.

While you could stay in your apartment after a major collapse by sheltering in place, it wouldn't be advisable. Your door and lock system are most likely cheaply built and so are your windows. In a post-collapse situation, you would have desperate neighbors and looters crawling all over your complex. This is why it is imperative to have a well-planned exit strategy by car and foot. Know where to stop for water and to rest, and obviously have a destination in mind that will get you away from the city.

Stay Insured

This last point should be common sense, but it is still worth mentioning. Make sure that all of your items, especially those with a high-dollar amount, are covered by your renter's insurance policy. Keep receipts, photos, and good records of what you own so that if your apartment is destroyed in a natural disaster or fire you can get reimbursed. Sometimes insurance companies have dollar limits on what can be claimed when it comes to valuable personal property or guns. Make sure to read your policy and know what is covered and what is not. It would be terrible to lose $10,000 worth of guns in an apartment fire, only to find out that your policy will only cover you up to $2,500.

16
AVOIDING MISTAKES

Single-Event Preparedness

The number one mistake in preparing is to focus all of your time and resources in preparing for a single event.

Multiple events may occur that are not related to what someone may be preparing for currently. Being prepared is about being able to survive any and all situations.

Given the state of the world today, multiple threats can present themselves over an extended period of time. These threats could be such things as natural disasters, civil unrest, economic collapse, or war. Survival tools and supplies are not "crisis specific." Focus on what will continuously be needed, regardless of the type of crisis.

You have probably watched the reality TV show, Doomsday Preppers, which depicts individuals and families that are preparing for a specific kind of disaster. While it is understood that preparing for a nuclear catastrophe, for instance, makes for good television, it may not always be the most practical way to prepare.

For instance, you may invest considerable finances into the equipment, supplies, and tools needed just to survive a nuclear blast, but what then? You still have to survive the days to come; this is where true survival skills come into play.

The facts are, regardless of how well prepared you are, if you are close enough to the blast area, you will not survive. If you are far enough away, you can survive without any special equipment or supplies. It is the area in between that is of greatest concern. Therefore, you must do a threat assessment to determine if you should prepare for this type of crisis at all, and if you feel that you don't fall in the "in between" zone, then focusing on disaster preparedness in general is a wiser choice.

Putting All Your Eggs in One Basket

Individuals and families tend to put all of their eggs in one basket, if you will.

People have literally built fortresses and have stockpiled a years' worth of supplies at one location. They may be convinced that no matter what happens, they will always be able to shelter-in-place. They may have put too much faith in their own preparedness, because even a single event can force them out of their location. There is only so much that can be carried off, so what happens to the supplies that are left behind?

This is why spreading your supplies out by having various caches around the area and having an alternative bug-out location are imperative. Gaining the necessary knowledge will allow you to survive away from your home. You need supplies, and in practical terms, you can never have too much, but you must always plan for the possibility of evacuation, so caching supplies should always be a part of any preparedness planning.

Physical Fitness

Your physical activity will increase during a crisis, and if you are not conditioned well enough now, you will find survival to be much more of a struggle than you may have initially expected.

You might be required to hump a heavy pack around after evacuating a disaster area, carrying with you supplies, tools, and materials to sustain life until it is safe to return home. You may have to flee with children on your back or help the elderly make their way through rubble and damaged structures. You will not be able to do any of this unless you are in relatively good shape. Your life and the life of others may depend on your physical readiness.

You may not be able to use motor vehicles because of damaged roads and lack of fuel. When is the last time you walked to the store and carried back bags of groceries? Could you do it if you had too?

Physical fitness must be a part of your survival plan. What good is it to have a bug-out-bag with all of that survival gear if you can't even get it past your city's limits, or even past the end of your street, for that matter?

Before starting any exercise program, you should first consult with your physician and have a checkup. You can't go from a relatively sedate lifestyle to one of extreme physical activity overnight. Even those that go to the gym two or three times a week may be in for a rude awakening. Walking for 10 miles over rough terrain with a 40-50 lb. pack on your back is very different from walking on a flat treadmill for 60 min. a few times a week. The only way to condition yourself for the activities required during a crisis is to emulate those same tasks on a consistent basis.

Not Knowing Why
Gathering what you think is needed and not knowing why you really need it is not a worthwhile venture. Knowing why you need the supplies, tools, and materials is as important as having the supplies themselves. Some people may research the Internet to figure out what they need, and while doing so, run across numerous prepping blogs that state the need of having one thing or another, but the blog may never really explain why that particular something is necessary to begin with. Ask yourself why a specific item is needed. Is someone simply trying to sell you something that may end up being pointless?

First, look around your home before purchasing anything, as you may find you already have that item or have something like it that may be used as a substitute for it.

Beware of Unguarded Talk

Talking too much about your plans, to possibly the wrong people, is an all too common mistake.

You have heard the old saying, "loose lips sink ships" (taken from a pamphlet distributed in World War II). This means that telling too many people, or the wrong person, your plans may have serious consequences during a disaster. On the one hand, you want to be able to help others and to share the knowledge and skills you are acquiring, but on the other hand, you are setting yourself up as a target, because too many people will know where to go when their lack of supplies has caught up to them. Some may ask, yet others may simply take.

The ones that halfheartedly started preparing because it seemed like the in-thing to do or because they felt pressured into it will be of main concern. Their hearts were never fully in it to begin with. They may have gathered a few supplies, but will unlikely know how to use many of them and will soon deplete what food and water they have. They had prepared, but they were not prepared. Your biggest threat, aside from the crisis itself, will come from citizens that live in and around your community.

Taking Inventory

How long have those canned goods been sitting on those shelves? Are your packaged grains free from weevils that may have bored through the packaging? Are your water bottles getting a little brittle to the touch? You will not have the answers to any of these questions unless you inspect your supplies regularly.

You should inventory your goods on a regular basis. Use and then replace any food items that may be close to expiration. Canned foods are usually useable for a few years past their expiration date, if stored in a cool, dark location; but be reminded that they will start to loose nutritional value as they age. Medical supplies and medications will have expiration dates as well.

You certainly do not want to find out that your supplies are no good after disaster strikes.

Buying Large Amounts
It should be obvious by now that the government is spying on everything that you do. Buying a ton of survival supplies from anywhere, all at once, is not a great idea, but especially when using a credit card or dealing with companies that are in the government's back pocket. You can avoid this by paying with cash when possible and only doing business with companies that respect your privacy.

Becoming Too Dependent on "Stuff"
Equipment degrades over time, tools break, and supplies run out. Does this mean that you will then stop surviving? It means that you should have a backup plan for your backup plan. You should learn more than one way to do such tasks as water filtration and purification. Have the tools and knowledge to dig a shallow well for emergency purposes, for example. Do not rely on any one tool or piece of equipment too much. Assume that things will malfunction and break, so that when

they inevitably do, you will have a constructive plan to fall back on.

Failing to Practice
Technology has done wonderful things for mankind, but it has also made all of us a little bit lazier. Have you ever watched an online video about primitive fire starting? Are you now convinced that you can start a fire by twirling the spindle on a fire board to create a coal, without ever having to get up from off your chair?

Would you build a car and sell it without test-driving it first? No! Would you serve a soup without tasting it beforehand? Of course not! So don't put your family at the mercy of an emergency plan that has never seen a drill before. The day your house catches on fire is not the day to learn how to escape a burning house; the day you have to evacuate is not the day to chart your route; and the day the blizzard strikes is not the day to stock up on food and water.

Many wannabe preppers buy a bunch of appealing gear and stop at that. Now that they have it, the novelty wears off, and they fail to ever use it again. I've seen it time and time again, with everything from freeze-dried foods to survival kits, and even with guns. If you can't act quickly and are not skilled with your supplies and gear, you might as well give it all away or sell it when the time comes. Be a survivalist, not a hoarder. Use your gear and your provisions until you become comfortable with them.

Your Plan/s

If you have a plan, you're at least a few steps ahead of the game already. However, it's extremely unlikely that your plan is perfect for every disaster scenario. Being unwilling to deviate from your plan could wind up getting you killed.

You can avoid this by having a main plan and a variety of back-up plans, for a variety of situations, and practicing the main plan and alternatives often. When rehearsing your plan/s, throw in a curve ball or two, which will force you to improvise and think about what you would do if part/s of your plan/s were to fail.

EDC

Leaving your EDC behind is like leaving your wallet or purse behind when going out the door in the morning. Just like the name implies, you're supposed to carry it with you "every day," wherever you go. If it's too bulky and too inconvenient to lug around, trim it back or alter your carry method.

Obsessed with Survival

Let's be clear, a healthy, happy family is more important than extending your food stock another month. Everything in the family begins with the husband and wife relationship. Make sure that's solid above all else, and everything else will fall into place. You will never be completely prepared for every scenario, no matter how hard you try. That is why attempting this will only result in burnout and may even make you think about giving up. Remember, God is ultimately in control, not you!

Conclusion

Our great-grandparents didn't have a name for "preparing;" they just called it "living." My great-grandparents never ate a chicken they hadn't raised themselves. They had a garden and "put up" food every year. They mended clothes. They made scarves out of worn out sweaters.

Although it's impractical to completely alter your way of life and return to the way the generations of old lived (back then, 90% of the population was rural; now 90% is urban or suburban), you can still possess a form of their readiness and develop a hardy state-of-mind that they were known for. The only thing that has to change fundamentally is this: You need to regain a certain degree of self-reliance and reliance on reliable resources. Since your family can't count on FEMA; they have to count on you. Don't disappoint them!

17
K-9 SURVIVAL

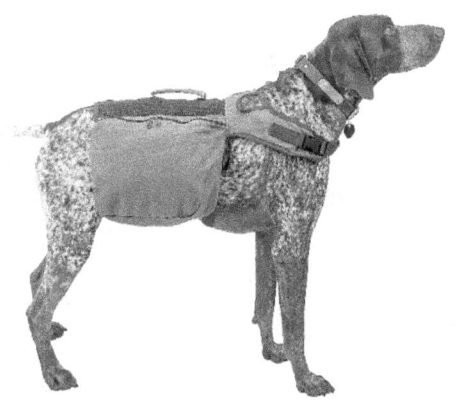

I would imagine that for most of us, when pondering emergency preparedness, quite naturally become fixated on the nuclear family. How can the wife, kids, and I make it out alive? Well, that is all fine and dandy if you are not part of the 137.2 million pet dog owners in North America; but if you are, then you are probably going to want to make provisions for Fido as well. You may feel that in doing so, you will be wasting valuable resources that you and your family could use instead, but think again. Consider all of the assets that your furry friend has to offer: excellent early warning/security system, close quarters fighting advantage, threat deterrent, and companionship. He could also be used as your emergency, "last resort" supply of food (let's assume that if you are reading this book, you will have prepared adequately enough that this need not ever be the case).

A few things that we will discuss in this chapter are how your dog's supplies should be carried if you need to evacuate on foot, what your dog will need during a bug-out situation, and how to start training your dog for this purpose.

C-BOB (Canine Bug-Out Bag)

I know this may sound funny, but yes, there is such a thing as a "canine bug-out bag." Why carry all of Fido's things on top of your own? Let him do some of the work, assuming he isn't a toy poodle, of course. Even if your furry friend can't fit everything into his pack for the journey, at least you are carrying less than you would be otherwise.

Types of Packs

In an ideal scenario your dog is big enough to carry his own bug-out bag. If this isn't the case, you'll simply need to incorporate his items into your own bug-out backpack. Dog packs made specifically for mobile hydration hold a few items that are great for trail runs or shorter day hikes. Other packs are made specifically for training and exercise. The best packs, however, for bugging out, will have more volume and extra padding to provide comfort on your dog's frame. If you have a large breed, the first thing you should do is buy a good saddle-bag dog backpack. The Outward Hound Backpack by Kygen is the ideal carrier. It's large, rugged, and built to be comfortable on your pets back.

Alternatively, if you plan to use your dog's backpack for more than just emergency situations, you might want something heavier duty like the Ruffwear Palisades Pack. It includes removable saddle bags, meaning you're able to let your dog rest without removing the harness. It also includes two built-in, collapsible, 1L hydration bottles to carry all of your dog's water.

Consider a waterproof pack if there's a chance you'll be in a lot of rain or snow. Also, consider a pack that is reflective and even has a spot to place a light. This really helps out with visibility at night or on foggy mornings.

Pack Features
All packs are designed to provide adequate weight distribution for your pet. Other common features include:

- **Dividers:** So that you can keep food and water separate from any other supplies.

- **Collapsible food dish:** Fits perfectly inside the pack or sometimes zips on the outside.

- **Pocket for a cooling insert:** You keep the cold pack in your freezer and insert it into the pack before heading out—great for hot climates. Improvise now, while you perform mock bug-outs, as you could certainly tie the cold pack to something immovable, next to a stream, and then let the cold pack sit in the water until nice and cold.

- **Top handle:** Makes it easy to hang onto your dog if you're crossing a shallow river or up onto a small ledge.

Additional Gear

This is just the beginning of the gear you can invest in to make the outdoors a safe place for your dog. A few other examples include:

- **A dog harness** for more technical trails or climbing.

- **A GPS beacon** and leash that fasten to you via carabiners.

- **A dog-specific bike trailer** (assuming that you are bugging out on a bike).
- **A dog tent** (Not all dogs like these for overnights, but they can double as sun shelters.)

- **Various types of leashes** (A waist-belt system is hand's free—nice when running; use a leash that can be clipped to your pack when hiking.)
- **A cooling collar** for hot days.

- **Creams** that help breeds that don't need boots stay comfortable in the snow.

How to Fit a Pack

Your first step in fitting your dog to his pack is to measure the circumference of your dog's chest. Most packs will have a specific chest size on the label so you can find the corresponding measurement in order to provide a general fit for dogs of different breeds and sizes. Place the middle of the pack on your dog's back. Straps usually fasten around the waist, chest and/or around the neck. Adjust all straps by tightening them in order to fit the pack to your dog's body. Next, fasten the plastic clamp in the middle of the dog's chest, making sure not to catch any fur in the process. Finally, adjust the clamp's strap to tighten the backpack by pulling the strap until you can snugly fit your pinkie between the pack and your dog's chest. This will allow enough room for your dog to move and breathe comfortably, but will keep the pack from slipping off. Repeat these steps with the pack's bottom strap. A pack that is improperly fitted can create significant discomfort for your dog: Too tight, and the pack may begin to chafe painfully as your dog moves about on the trail. Too loose, and the objects inside the pack may shift, throwing the pack off-centre and your dog off-balance.

Doggy Supplies

Water
Just like in a human BOB, clean water is one of the most important things that you can pack for your dog. Dogs need about one ounce of water, per pound of body weight, per day. One gal. of water weighs 10 lbs., so a 70-lb. Golden Retriever would need a minimum of 70 oz. of water per day. One gal. of water is 128 oz. In this example, you'd be carrying a little more than 5 lbs. of water for your dog's consumption, for a one-day period. Since water is heavy and dogs are susceptible to Giardia protozoa like in humans, you must also include ways to disinfect and filter whatever water you come across. You can't realistically expect to carry all the water your dog will need longer term. You will certainly need a container for this purpose, but I wouldn't add the extra weight for a doggy canteen, when you can just use your own container for this purpose, especially when you will just be pouring the clean water into his dish anyway. In

this way you save space, decrease weight, and eliminate the risk of germ transferal.

Collapsible Water/Food Bowl
Now that you have your water, you're going to need something to serve it in. The best option for a dog on the go is a collapsible water dish. It's reliable, has a pull string to keep food in if necessary, and folds up nice and small for easy storage.

Electrolyte Source
Dogs find themselves in need of electrolytes just like their human counterparts do. Don't expect your own supply to cover both of you; always have

a separate supply for your dog. Make sure it is not loaded with sugar. (Refer back to the "H2O" chapter of this book.)

Food
The next thing you'll need to include in your dog's bug-out bag is food. Consider that during a strenuous trip or bug-out, your dog is going to need more calories, possibly even double what you are used to feeding him on a regular basis. Check with your vet to ensure your dog will be getting the right amount of calories for the estimated energy that will be expended on your possible bug-out route. Your vet is also a great resource to advise upon the exercise level that is right for your dog.

Some recommend freeze-dried or dehydrated dog food in order to keep the weight down. There are brands out there that are happy to sell you their product, but remember that whenever you feed any new food to your pet for the first time, it is best to transition slowly. Mix increasing amounts of your pet's new food with decreasing amounts of the previous food over a 7 to 14 day period. That is why a survival situation, especially with the added stress that comes along with it, is not the time to be doing this. If you think that you are going to want to go this route, then you will need to test-run this approach and start switching over your dog to this new food NOW. If you and your dog are happy with his dog food of choice at this present time and you don't want to switch to lighter fare, then you need to take that extra weight into consideration for your or your dog's pack.

Leash and Long Cordage

Next up on the list of "must haves" is a short leash to keep your dog close and under-control. Remember to also pack a bit of long cordage in order to tie your dog up at night, while leaving him enough room to patrol the camp. If you packed a proper human BOB, your kit should already include 550 paracord, which will suffice for both you and your dog.

Medication

Just like with a human BOB, don't fail to pack your C-BOB with your pup's medications. Although many preparedness websites recommend a 3-day supply, I recommend at least a one-week supply. It is better to have more medication than needed rather than less, especially if these medications could mean the difference between life and death.

Sleeping Gear

Depending on what the weather is going to be like, if you have a short-haired dog, you may want to consider sleeping gear if temperatures drop below 50 °F.

Some dog enthusiasts opt for kid's sleeping bags, while others carry ultralight, 2-person sleeping bags so that they can snuggle with their pooch when the temperature drops very low. It all depends on your pup, the breed, and learning what he needs in order to be comfortable. Attempt a campout with your dog in cooler weather in order to know what makes your furry pal cozy.

When it's raining, let your dog rest on his mat under the rainfly until he has dried off a bit. Sleeping is no fun when you're a sopping wet dog, especially when it's going to get chilly.

Dog Clothing
In addition to sleeping gear, give some thought to your dog's attire. Indoor dogs and breeds with thin coats can benefit from an outer layer to preserve body temperature in cold, wet conditions.

If it's likely that you will be bugging-out in a very hot environment, you might consider a dog vest.

You can soak it with water to dissipate heat as the water evaporates. On the other temperature extreme, consider a fleece bodysuit that covers your dog's entire body and legs. This suit is probably unnecessary when your dog is working hard during the day, but your dog will likely appreciate PJs when it's frosty at night. In fact, some dogs do just fine with an extra layer and no sleeping bag at night.

It may seem like overkill, but a dog coat is another good investment for those nippy days or nights, especially to protect your dog's underside when going backpacking in the snow.

Neoprene Dog Shoes
The notion of having your dog wear doggy boots may sound a little ridiculous, and your dog may even act confused the first time he is adorned in footwear, but Fido will give you a big lick out of gratitude when the time comes for him to wear them.

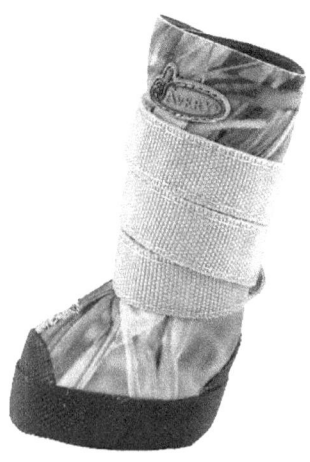

If you're planning on moving on foot for any long distances, it's good to have a spare pair of neoprene dog shoes available. Buy a pair of rugged boots made to last on rough terrain where rocks or other objects might cut into your dog's pads. These dog boots also work well at protecting your dog's paws from the elements, such as from the cold and wet caused by snow and rain, and even from the heat radiated by a rock face, for instance, when it is sunny and above 70°F . Even the salt used on icy sidewalks during the winter is very irritating to a dog's paws.

It may take you a few tries before you find the right pair that doesn't fall off as your dog tromps through the snow. It is recommended that you test out your dog's boots on short walks and hikes before he goes on a big trip. This may end up being one of your dog's least favorite items, so just like with the canine BOB, make sure you get your dog used to wearing these well in advance of any emergency situation.

Muzzle

While it pains most responsible dog owners to see their pup with a muzzle on, it very well could save the life of both you and your dog. Trust me, if there is ever a time when a bark could get you both killed, it will be during a bug-out situation.

Pet First Aid

Be prepared. Sites such as peteducation.com have a lot of good information about dogs, including many articles about first aid. Petco and the Red Cross offer first-aid classes in order to give you the hands-on training that you will need.

Much like a human first-aid kit, the contents of one customized for your pet can be feverishly debated. If you're like most people, however, you may prefer to buy one rather than put one together from scratch. Luckily, there are a lot of pre-built kits out there to choose from, including the Mayday First Aid Kit for Pets, which comes with pretty much everything you will need, including antibiotic ointment, splinter removers, examination gloves, and a pet first-aid guide—a pretty good steal for under $20.

Nail Clippers and Hair Brush
If you're doing any reasonable amount of bush-whacking once you're out of Dodge, your dog is going to get a lot of debris stuck in his fur. In addition to a quality-made dog brush and comb, a good pair of nail clippers can make all the difference in your pooch's comfort level.

Doggy Waste Bags
OK … OK … OK, I know what you're saying, "If it's the end of the world, why should I care where my dog goes number 2?" Well, maybe the better question is why wouldn't you want to prevent disease? You must remember that your dog's waste is raw sewage and contains harmful bacteria and parasites, such as Salmonella, Giardia, E. coli, and roundworms.

You certainly want your bug-out location to stay a clean, sanitary environment. Rather than track doggy doo-doo around or let it seep into groundwater, bury it just as you would human waste--at least 200 feet away from trails, camps, and water sources. Another option, of course, would be to scoop it up using a doggy waste bag.

Collapsible Dog Crate (optional)

Many dog owners will suggest having a collapsible crate that you can strap on to your own bag. The principle is very sound--having a portable shelter for your own dog to hide in is incredibly valuable in almost every situation. If you don't mind the extra weight, then definitely consider investing in one.

Toys

Of course, if you are trying to save the space, a dog toy will be the first thing that you will want to eliminate, but if your dog has a favorite toy that he plays with every single day, then it might not hurt to make room for it, as this will give him some familiarity and fun during a bug-out scenario.

Recap List

So that's everything you need to keep your pet happy and healthy in any emergency situation. For those looking for a quick list, I'll recap below:

- Dog backpack
- Water
- Collapsible water/food bowl
- Electrolyte solution
- Food
- Leash and long cordage
- Medication
- Sleeping gear
- Dog clothing
- Neoprene dog shoes
- Muzzle
- Pet first-aid kit
- Nail clippers and hair brush
- Doggy waste bags
- Collapsible dog crate (optional)
- Favorite dog toy (dogs are like children)

- Pet's vaccination records and registration (in case you need to gain access to a shelter)

Is Your Dog Physically Ready?

Whatever pack you choose, the most important thing you can do is get your dog used to wearing it. Ease your dog into the routine of hiking and wearing a pack. Start off by having him wear a pack around the house, then on short walks, then on longer walks.

You should also start with an empty pack and then slowly move from lighter loads to heavier ones. This will help your dog become comfortable with wearing a new backpack, and then you can slowly work your way up to a full bag. In general, young and healthy dogs can carry up to 25% of their weight. Some breeds can carry 10–15% more, while other breeds aren't cut out to carry much at all. The amount you should pack also changes with age. For dogs that are older or in poor physical condition, discuss the safety of exercise and wearing a pack with your vet.

C-BOB for Redundancies
Your dog's bug-out bag can have redundancy items for you as well. I plan on packing my black lab, Luke, with an extra SAS survival pouch, a blowout first-aid kit, a 9mm handgun, and a couple of loaded magazines. Who knows, one day he may save my neck. He is impossible to catch and only listens to my commands—some marauders may get my pack and other supplies, but Luke will come back to me when the opportunity arises, putting me back into the game. This may be more fantasy

than reality, but in theory, it seems like a good back-up plan.

Toy and Small Breeds
Let me quickly interject a few remarks regarding toy and small breeds. As you probably know, the toy breeds will NOT be carrying a pack of any kind and neither of these breeds will be able to walk the long distances that their medium and large counterparts will. The best options for these pups are pet-sling carriers or front-carrier backpacks—think baby slings or baby carriers. These are handy for when your pup poops out. Either of these nifty devices will keep you and your dog trudging forward. These will also be useful for geriatric or sickly toy and small breed dogs.

Dog Carts
Well, we have covered dog saddle bags, pet-sling carriers, and front-carrier backpacks for pets so far. These three methods entail carrying, but how about pulling? If you are so inclined, assuming that your pooch is healthy enough, let him pull his belongings rather than carry them—think sledding, but rather than a sled, a cart on wheels. Basically, your dog will be wearing a harness that protects your dog from injury by distributing weight around the shafts that pull a basket on wheels.

Just like with the C-BOB, you will have to invest some time and energy by way of training your dog to use this contraption. Some dogs will love it from the start and others will take a few lessons in order to get the hang of it. Your dog will certainly need some basic obedience training, since you will use voice commands to steer your dog. Alternately, you can attach leashes to the harness as reins or a head halter can also be used. Using treats as an incentive will encourage your dog to move forward. There are a plethora of draft-dog resources online as well. Essentially, the learning to cart steps will include the following:

- Basic obedience
- Carting commands
- Getting used to the harness
- Getting used to pulling something
- Getting used to being around the cart
- Learning to accept the shafts
- Learning to stand to be hitched
- Pulling the cart
- Maneuvering

If you have a pulling-breed dog, such as a Siberian Husky, an Alaskan Malamute, a Bernese Mountain Dog, a Greater Swiss Mountain Dog, a Great Pyrenees, a herding dog, a bully breed, a Dobe, or a Rottie, then you are already one step ahead, as these breeds probably already know how to pull!

You may be wondering how much weight your dog will be able to pull. Dogs in good condition can comfortably pull 2-3 times their body weight over moderate to long distances. Off-road and extremely hilly terrain will reduce this by one-third to half. Every dog is different, so be patient and make allowances as needed. Hey, your dog may end up totally surprising you if you truly make this a hobby or way of life. I'm sure that you have heard of weight pulling as a dog sport. Many breeds participate in this sport, with dogs being separated into classes by weight. Depending on the size and breed of dog, hundreds, if not thousands of pounds, can be pulled by one dog alone!

It's up to you if you want to create your own setup or purchase a custom-made cart. A customized cart will of course save you a lot of work, but the cheapest that I could find online was $159 for the smallest size and $295 for a medium to large dog and these prices do not include the carting harness, which is sold separately. There are several different websites that offer resources on how to build your own shafts and cart. In that case, you would just purchase the harness separately.

At the End of the Day

At trip's end, be sure to check your dog's body for ticks, burrs, and other annoying objects. If you do find a tick, contact your vet, while there is one to be found (in an end-of-the-world scenario, this will most likely not be an option). There are different dangers for pets regionally, so a vet can help you decide if you should remove the tick yourself or come into the office. Also, wash your dog with some medicated shampoo, when necessary, as the plants that brush up against your dog can sometimes irritate his belly, especially if he doesn't have a lot of fur on it. However, most dogs will be fine with a regular, non-medicated bath.

18
SURVIVAL COMMUNICATIONS

Communication is a key element in our day to day lives. If you don't agree, challenge yourself by going a whole day with no cell/home phone, no Internet, no television, no radio, nor any other means of giving or receiving communication. So it stands to reason that having communication, when the world goes silent, is essential to gaining intelligence, to the safety and security of our families, to keeping informed, and to keeping at least one step ahead of anybody with bad intentions.

Unless your game plan is to be totally cut off during an emergency situation, which would be a HUGE disadvantage, you need at least some sort of rudimentary communication system. At the very least, some sort of receiver system is necessary. Depending on the situation, you may need information on how to take shelter (inclement weather), how to leave an area (terrorist, chemical spill, etc.), or on many other considerations.

Your options are basically one-way or two-way communication. One way consists of AM/FM radio, television, shortwave radio, Internet websites, other radio services, etc. Two-way communication consists of SSB/CW/digital radio on ham bands and other radio services, cell/home phones, satellite phones, email, Facebook, instant messaging, etc.

Communication Options

It is recommended that you have at least three options of distance communication. We will take a look at some of the advantages, as well as disadvantages, of several survival communication options, including smart phones with apps, standard walkie-talkies (GMRS/FRS), police scanners, and ham radios. Knowing what is going on around you, in your city, during survival situations will keep you one step ahead of the rest.

Smartphone

No one knows exactly how many little plastic handsets there are in the world, but the best guess is over 4.6 billion. That's around two thirds of the planet's population! In developing countries, where large-scale land line networks (ordinary telephones wired to the wall) are few and far between, over 90 percent of the phones in use are cellphones. Cellphones (also known as cellular phones and, chiefly in Europe, as mobile phones or mobiles) are radio telephones that route their calls through a network of masts linked to the main public telephone network. Yes, at its most basic, a cell phone is a radio—an extremely sophisticated radio, but a radio nonetheless.

The genius of the cellular system is the division of a city into small cells. This allows extensive frequency reuse across a city, so that millions of people can use cell phones simultaneously.

Suppose you're in the middle of a big city and millions of people are all calling at once. In this case, you'd need just as many millions of separate frequencies—more than are usually available. The solution is to divide the city up into smaller areas, with each one served by its own masts and base station. These areas are what we call cells, and they look like a patchwork of invisible hexagons. Each cell consists of a tower and a small building containing the radio equipment. All the calls made or received inside that cell are routed through them. Cells enable the system to handle many more calls at once, because each cell uses the same set of frequencies as its neighboring cells.

The more cells, the greater the number of calls can be made at once. This is why urban areas have many more cells than rural areas and why the cells in urban areas are much smaller.

A simple call is if a phone in cell A calls a phone in cell B. The call doesn't pass directly between the phones, but from the first phone to mast A and its base station, then to mast B and its base station, and then to the second phone.

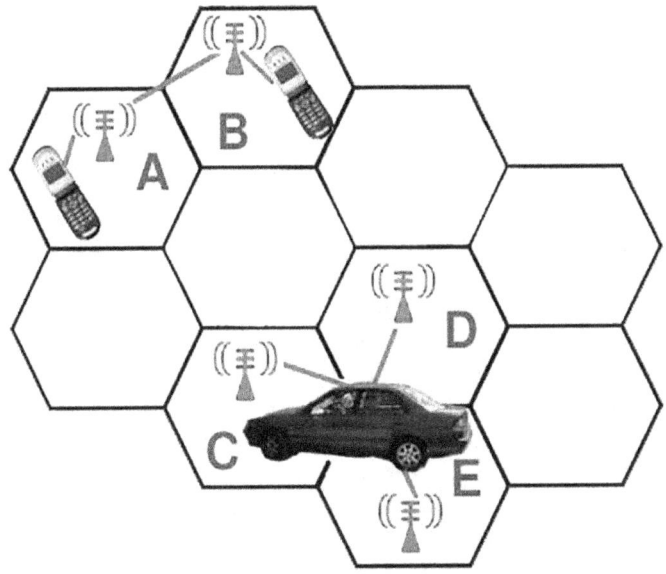

If a car passenger is making a roaming call and the car drives between cells C, D, and E, the phone call is automatically "handed off" (passed from cell to cell) so the call is not interrupted.

The key to understanding cells is to realize that cellphones and the masts they communicate with are designed to send radio waves only over a limited range; that effectively defines the size of the cells. It's also worth pointing out that this picture is a simplification; it's more accurate to say that the masts sit at the intersections of the cells, but it's a little easier to understand things as they have been shown.

Brace yourselves, my friends. Although a mobile/

cell phone is a type of two-way radio, if the power goes out, you won't be able to Google what to do in a grid-down scenario. Yes, we know all your smartphones and cool tablets are wireless, but with any glitch in the power grid, routers and transmitters will go down immediately. However, there are things you can do with your cell phone if you have your Wi-Fi or data connection. You can use apps like a scanner app. Apps on a phone are great, but keep in mind that you will need a Wi-Fi signal or a data connection. If you bug out to the woods or the 3G or 4G goes down, you will lose this capability. Some apps require a data connection and some do not. In addition to things like GPS for navigation and weather apps for the forecast, one of the cool ones that I like is scanner radio, which can be downloaded from the Apple Store or Android Market. It's a great way to find out what's going on around you: local police, fire, traffic, or city-wide services. Since its broadcast through the Internet, you can listen to anything that is going on around the country (your distance to the repeater is irrelevant). The two downsides are Internet connection may be unavailable and smartphone batteries die quickly with heavy use.

With the emergence of smartphones into our daily lives, it only makes sense to have multiple preparedness applications specific for EDC purposes. A variety of mobile apps exist that mimic a walkie-talkie style interaction. Applications on the market that offer this walkie-talkie style interaction for audio include Voxer, Zello, and HeyTell, among others. An application that offers this style of interaction for video is Glide.

Here is a list of apps that I have found useful in an urban environment.

- Google Goggles
- Glympse
- GasBuddy
- CamScanner
- Maps With Me
- Scanner Radio
- Hiker
- Disaster Alert
- First Aid (Red Cross)
- iTriage
- SAS Survival Guide (Lite)
- WeatherBug
- The Weather Channel
- Magnifying Glass
- 4D Compass
- Smart Ruler
- Bubble (Level)
- Max Unit Converter
- White Pages
- WiGLE Wifi
- Translate
- WiFi File Transfer

Pros

- No limit on range of communication
- Texting
- Internet
- Apps
- Easy to use
- Small enough to fit in your pocket

Cons

- Only works with paid service
- Limited to no reception in places you would need it most

- If there is any glitch in the power grid, routers and transmitters will go down immediately, especially in an emergency.
- Battery life is short-lived.
- Cannot use common-size batteries, like AA and AAA

Listen Only (Receivers)

Receivers are radios that receive radio signals but cannot transmit them. Below is a breakdown of the two most common types of radio receivers.

Radio Scanner

The air around you is bursting with radio waves. You know that you can flip on the AM/FM radio in your car and receive dozens of stations. You can flip on a CB radio and receive 40 more. You can flip on a TV and receive many broadcast channels. Cell phones can send and receive hundreds of frequencies. This is just the tip of the radio-spectrum iceberg. Literally tens of thousands of other radio broadcasts and conversations are whizzing past you as you read this—police officers, firefighters, ambulance drivers, paramedics, sanitation workers, space-shuttle astronauts, race-car drivers, and even babies with their monitors are transmitting radio waves all around you at this very moment!

To tap into this ocean of electromagnetic dialogue and hear what all of these people are talking about, all you need is a scanner. A scanner is basically a radio receiver capable of receiving multiple signals. Generally, scanners pick up signals in the VHF to UHF range.

Scanners typically operate in three modes

- Scan
- Manual Scan
- Search

In scan mode, the receiver constantly changes frequencies in a set order looking for a frequency that has someone transmitting. Lights or panel-mounted displays show what channel or frequency is in use as the scanner stops on a given frequency. The frequencies can be preprogrammed on some models or manually set on practically all models. However, scanners must be programmed to scan the correct frequencies or else they will just be expensive paperweights.

In manual-scan mode, the user taps a button or turns a dial to manually step through preprogrammed frequencies one frequency at a time.

In search mode, the receiver is set to search between two sets of frequencies within a given band. This mode is useful when a user does not know a frequency, but wants to know what frequencies are active in a given area. If the frequency the scanner stops at during a search is interesting, the user can store that frequency in the radio scanner and use it in scan mode.

Scanners are gaining popularity with consumers and most are very portable and affordable.

Some of the recently released scanners are capable of tracking municipalities and police frequencies in the 800-megahertz (MHz) range. This is known as trunk tracking of computer-controlled trunked radio networks.

Higher-end scanners can be controlled by the serial port of a personal computer using special software. This helps the user with the logging of stations as well as with duplicating the scanner controls within the software application.

Many models receive the NOAA weather radio broadcasts. This can be a very useful feature during impending tornadoes or hurricanes.

Radio scanners usually come with small whip antennas as well as an external antenna connector. An outside antenna or attic antenna enables you to hear more transmissions at a greater distance.

Scanners cannot hear everything. The typical consumer-grade scanner cannot listen in on 900-MHz cordless phones that use digital spread spectrum (DSS) technology. Analog cell phone frequencies are also blocked by law on all scanners.

Some law enforcement agencies also use audio inversion and other scrambling technologies to prevent the reception of sensitive communications. You will not be able to decipher these conversations. One downfall of standard scanners is that they cannot scan digital frequencies. Law enforcement is making the switch to digital and encrypted communications, which could make the typical scanner obsolete in your area for monitoring these services. Digital scanners are available, but are much more expensive at the moment. Some law enforcement and emergency agencies also operate on frequencies above the range supported by most scanner models.

Even so, there is an UNBELIEVABLE number of radio services that use frequencies most scanners can hear.

Scanner Tips
Once you buy a scanner, read the manual from cover to cover so you know all of its capabilities. Ask questions in one of the many scanner newsgroups on the Internet—there are active USENET newsgroups that many scanner hobbyists visit. You can use *rec.radio.scanner* or *alt.radio.scanner*, which are easily accessed through your Web browser. Check out some of the scanning resources on the Internet, and then try these tips:

- Become a frequency collector. Start with index cards or perhaps a small database program on your computer. Learn how to do searches within a given band—search a 1-MHz segment at a time and record the compelling frequencies you find.
- Consider finding a way to run your radio from emergency power if you have a desktop model. That way, you can listen to police and fire crews during power failures and severe weather. Typically, a very small 12-volt battery is all that is needed.
- Consider storing frequencies of a similar type all in the same bank. That way, if you

just want to listen to police, fire, or aviation, you can scan just the frequency memory bank you're interested in and "lockout" the others.

- Take your scanner on a trip and listen from the hotel or motel room.
- Take your scanner to all sporting events where radios are used.
- Listen to local amateur radio operators at 144 -148 MHz. Volunteer, ham-radio spotters are often heard during a weather watch or a weather warning.
- Until you buy your own scanner, you can try out scanning frequencies on Web-controlled receivers.
- You can find out what frequencies are used locally on *http://www.radioreference.com/apps/db/*
- Go to *StupidScannerTricks.com*, *StrongSignals.net*, or *http://www.bearcat1.com/free.htm* for scanner frequencies and codes.

Pros

- Receives info from local sources during an emergency, such as weather, traffic, fire, ambulance, police, etc.
- Has the capability of scanning channels automatically, so that you don't have to spend time searching manually.
- Most can use common-size batteries, like AA and AAA.

Cons

- Only expensive models can receive digital signals

- Cannot pick up encrypted communications that some law-enforcement agencies use
- Are typically complicated and require manual programming of your local frequencies before the device will be effective

Shortwave Radio

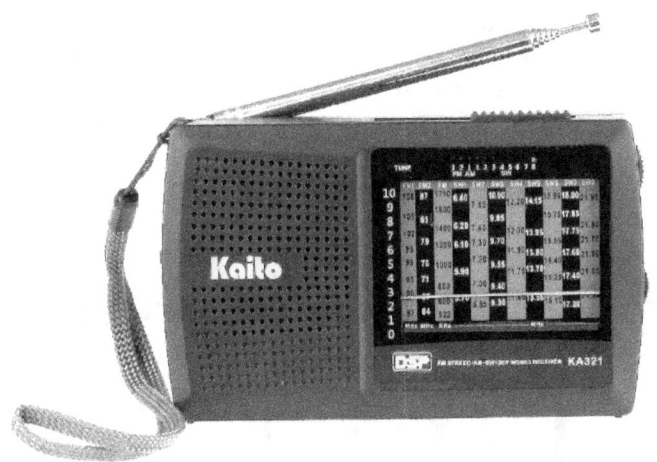

Shortwave radio picks up a unique band of long distance frequencies. You can listen in on news that is broadcast from around the world using a shortwave radio, which could be extremely important in a major disaster. If local communications are taken out, a shortwave radio could fill you in on what is going on from sources on the outside.

Shortwave radios also usually have AM/FM capability so it could replace your standard radio.

Pros

- Inexpensive
- Can receive info from around the world
- Can receive standard AM/FM in most cases

Cons

- Cannot pick up local frequencies (emergency, police, HAM, CB, FRS/GMRS)

Two-Way Radios (Transceivers)

Two-way radios are simply radios that can be used to both transmit and receive. The frequencies that a two-way radio can operate on determine if a radio is considered a HAM radio, a walkie talkie, CB radio, etc. Below is a breakdown of the common types of two-way radios.

Standard Walkie Talkie (GMRS/FRS)

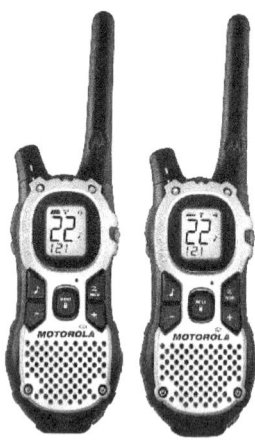

The next-step-up in survival communication, two-way radios (in this case, we are not talking about cell phones, but group-call communication) are available at pretty much any sporting-goods store, on Amazon, at Wal-Mart, etc. In broader terms, most voice-wireless-communications systems fall into the two-way radio definition.

This two-way radio system is also known as Professional Mobile Radio (PMR), Land Mobile Radio (LMR), Private Mobile Radio (PMR), or Public Access Mobile Radio (PAMR) system. Two-way radios usually come in a combo pack and work off The Family Radio Service (FRS)/General Mobile Radio Service (GMRS), so you don't need a license to operate them. A quality, two-way radio pair will cost you under $100. Two-way radios are transceivers (they send and receive signals) and utilize the push-to-talk system. Walkie-talkies, as they were called, were first developed for military use during World War II and eventually spread to public and commercial use after the war. The first radio receiver/transmitter to be widely nicknamed "Walkie-Talkie" was the *backpacked* Motorola SCR-300, created by an engineering team in 1940 at the Galvin Manufacturing Company (fore-runner of Motorola). Motorola also produced the hand-held AM SCR-536 radio during World War II, and it was called the "Handie-Talkie" (HT). The terms are often confused today, but the original walkie-talkie referred to the back mounted model, while the handie-talkie was the device which could be held entirely in the hand (but had vastly reduced performance).

Two-way radios have come a long way since those bygone days, but their old-fashioned nicknames are still in use today. The abbreviation HT, derived from Motorola's "Handie Talkie" trademark, is commonly used to refer to portable, handheld ham radios, with "walkie-talkie" often used as a layman's term or specifically to refer to a toy. Public safety or commercial users generally refer to their handhelds simply as "radios."

Two-way radio provides instant communication. Users just need to press the "push-to-talk" (PTT) button and within a fraction of a second, this user can immediately talk and convey their messages. Another distinct feature of two-way radio is its capability to facilitate "one-to-many" group communication (also known as "group call") very efficiently. This means that one user can talk to one, five, ten, one hundred, and even thousands of users at the same time. Users don't need to repeat the same message over and over again. In addition, two-way radio performs the group communication using minimum RF channel resources. If all of the users reside in the same area most of the time, you only need one channel resources to talk to these hundreds of users.

Some of the frequencies are Family Radio Services (FRS) frequencies, which automatically limit the amount of power that the device uses when transmitting to a power output of half a watt. The disadvantage with this is that it limits the range/clarity of the device to up to 6 miles in ideal conditions, but on the flip side, you can transmit on these frequencies without any type of license. Essentially, FRS is a free service for short-range use. The FRS band sparked the two-way radio popularity explosion. It was created by the FCC in

1996, with 7 channels provided specifically for two-way radio users. FRS users can also use the 7 shared channels with GMRS for a total of 14 channels, provided you broadcast using the maximum half-watt of power.

Inevitably, consumers wanted more power, greater range, and more channels. Manufacturers responded by introducing recreational radios that also used the General Mobile Radio Service (GMRS) band. Originally allocated for commercial use, GMRS offers 8 additional channels plus the 7 shared GMRS/FRS channels for a total of 22 channels. Though GMRS technically allows a maximum power output of 50 watts (used for base stations), most recreational hand-helds offer 1 or 2 watts to keep size and weight low. If there are GMRS repeaters in your area (basically towers that amplify your transmission), you will be able to communicate at much greater distances. It is possible to buy 5-watt, handheld, programmable radios and program them to use GMRS frequencies. This would extend the range of the radio further than pre-programmed consumer versions.

To operate a radio that uses GMRS channels, a 5-year family license is available from the FCC for $85. The good thing about a GMRS license is that there is no test and your entire family is allowed to use the GMRS frequencies when you buy one license. You do not need a license before purchasing a GMRS-capable, two-way radio. Go to *www.fcc.gov* for more information on licensing (Form 605).

Most radios offer 22 channels and up to 121 privacy (or interference-elimination) codes for each main channel. Out of those channels, you can use 7 of them without a license. They are great for camping, hiking, skiing, car-to-car communication, and a bug-out situation. The main disadvantage is their lack of communications at a wide range. Their advertised range is 25-30 miles, give or take, in ideal conditions, but you will never be able to get anywhere near that in an urban environment.

Regardless of a unit's published optimal range, in roughly 90% of situations, a radio's actual range will be about 2 miles or less. Several factors can inhibit two-way radio performance:

- Topography (hills, deep canyons, ridgelines, tall formations)
- Weather (such as thick clouds)
- Electromagnetic interference (lightning)
- Obstructions (dense forest, structures)
- Large metal surfaces (inside a vehicle, range is usually less than 1 mile)

The human body (which is dense and watery) can also block radio waves. You may boost reception of incoming signals if you attach a radio to a section of your pack that remains away from your body instead of clipping it to your belt.

Potential causes of radio interference are as random as nature itself. So yes, your two-way radio results may vary.

While dense forests or multiple ridgelines can be major impediments to radio signals, scattered trees and bushes are mostly transparent or "translucent" to these signals. Therefore, even in forested or hilly territory, two-way radios generally do a fair to good job of transmitting short-range signals.

A chief benefit of higher-powered radios (1- or 2-watt models) is their ability to fill in coverage dropouts (behind hills or buildings, for example) that often occur within the line of sight of a radio user. The higher power tends to improve the overall quality of the signal.

From a high vantage point looking down into a flat valley or lowland area with minimal tree cover on a clear day will give you the maximum range rating. Flat, obstruction-free settings are also good for transmitting radio signals, but the addition of height greatly boosts your range potential (for instance, a large lake with nearby hills—a setting where two-way radios are often tested). During such tests, three or more radio users may be deployed around a lake:

- On a boat
- On the lakeshore
- On a hilltop several hundred feet high

Depending on what type of radio is being used, the boat and lakeshore users can usually communicate at distances of 4-6 miles. The hilltop user and the boat user can potentially hit the top of a radio's range (if the lake is large enough and distant topography does not interfere).

From high vantage points—say, a 1,000ft. hill in the vicinity of a population center located below in an open valley—you may find a radio has *too much* range. It's possible you'll hear people talking on every channel. In such an ideal situation, even a half-watt radio could send its signal 25 miles or more.

Ultimately, a key rule for optimizing coverage is achieving good line of sight. You will increase your ability to increase your range as you increase the elevation of your position. Attaining a high point above an otherwise flat area can be a huge benefit toward optimizing your radio's maximum range.

Two-way radios have a vibrate feature, so you don't hear a beep, making them more stealthy. They also have hands-free headsets that are voice activated. I would recommend getting the models that have the NOAA—National Oceanic and Atmospheric Administration—radio built into them, both for your pack and for your whole family or group.

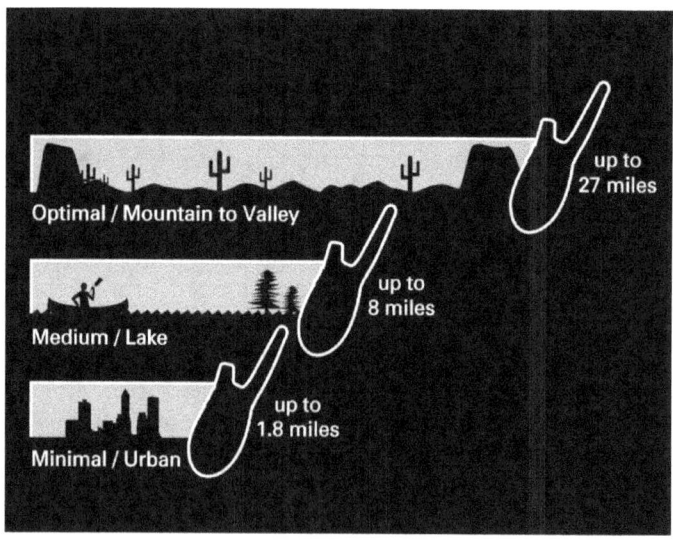

Unfortunately, you will be unable to listen in on police, fire, or government-type frequencies like the scanner-radio app on your cell phone. You are also limited to just the radio-to-radio channels built into them. Regardless of the limitations, two-way radios are still a great family-communication option.

Tips for Locating a Clear Channel

1. Switch off the radio's continuous tone coded squelch system (CTCSS).

2. Choose a channel and listen for activity. (Since many users do not bother to change channels, Channel 1 is usually busy.)

3. Listen for a minute or two. If conversations are ongoing, try Channel 2, then Channel 3, and so forth until an unused main channel is found. Unless you are in a high-traffic area (such as a ski resort), usually a vacant main channel can be located.

According to Roy Reese, chief product engineer of Giant International, a Georgia-based manufacturer of two-way radios that licenses products to a major electronics firm, there are multiple ways to express power and some of the numbers put on packages have nothing to do with a two-way radio's capabilities. Per Reese, "What really matters is an antenna's 'effective radiated power'—a measure of what's flying off the antenna. It doesn't matter how big the amplifier is. What's important is how effectively an antenna is radiating its power level."

Two-way radios, Reese explains, capture waves that are approximately 12.5 in. in length. "The effectiveness of the antenna is crucial in coupling with that power of the transmission, and generally a bigger antenna is better," he says. "But you have to consider how well a big antenna is going to fit in your backpack. Naturally, the people in industrial design want something small and sexy with a long range. You can't have both."

For two-way users hungry for peak power in a small unit, Reese suggests looking for radios with antenna and radio bodies of equal or near-equal lengths. "Think balanced," Reese says.

Compare Features When Determining What Two-Way Radio to Purchase

- Size, shape, and weight
- Calling and paging features
- Scanning
- Keypad lock
- VOX (voice-activated feature)
- Noise filter
- Weather radio
- Headset jacks
- Radio/GPS combo units

Other Considerations

- Batteries

Most two-way radios run on standard AA or AAA batteries. Others come with their own rechargeable NiMH (nickel-metal hydride) or NiCad (nickel-cadmium) battery packs. A few can accommodate either.

In general, the higher a radio's power output, the faster it will drain your batteries. Look for models that send the unit into a low-power, battery-saver mode after a certain amount of time has elapsed between broadcasts. Also consider a solar charger for in-the-field replenishment of NiMH and NiCad batteries.

- Compatibility

Any two-way radios broadcasting on the same frequency (FRS or GMRS) and supporting the same channels will work together. Keep in mind, though, that to get full use of your radio's other features, you'll need another radio with the same features. Thus, it makes sense to buy in pairs.

When people buy new radios, they are sometimes frustrated by their inability to connect with older radios. Since older radios cannot send out the number of tones that newer radios can, this can usually be solved by setting the new radio to channel 1, code 0. The default setting for new radios is channel 1, code 1.

This is explained in most user manuals. Here's something you should know about manuals: While it is natural to break out newly purchased two-way radios, insert batteries, and begin experimenting with them, it's a smart move to sit down and devote some time to reading the user manual thoroughly. You'll usually learn a pointer or two that will make operating your radios a simpler task.

Usage Area

As a side note, although probably a moot point at that, two-way radios made for use in the USA are generally not legal to use outside of North America. In 2005, the frequencies used for two-way radios in the United States and Canada were aligned, both meeting the same requirements. Mexico formally allocates only FRS channels. Other countries may use these frequencies for police, military, or other applications.

Pros

- Affordable to purchase
- Easy to use
- Compact/ much smaller and lighter than CB radios
- Can use repeaters on GMRS frequencies
- Potentially long ranges and excellent sound quality
- Operate anywhere in the U.S., no cell-phone coverage issues
- No monthly service
- Small power requirements
- Most can use common-size batteries, like AA and AAA

Cons

- Reception is limited to line-of-sight usage/no access to repeaters
- Requires an FCC license and fee to transmit on GMRS frequencies
- Clear channels can be difficult to find in congested areas

Bottom Line

For short-range use in uncrowded areas, FRS channels may be all that you need. For longer-range use and more channel options, you'll want GMRS channels. For ultimate convenience and versatility, choose one of the new radio/GPS units.

MURS Radio

Multi Use Radio Service (MURS) radios are similar in capabilities to FRS/GMRS radios. A different frequency band (made up of only 5 frequencies) is used. MURS radios are allowed to use more power to transmit than a radio transmitting on an FRS frequency but less power than a radio transmitting in a GMRS frequency. No license is required to transmit on MURS frequencies.

Pros

- Affordable
- Easy to use
- Compact
- Does not require a license

Cons

- Limited range
- Limited number of frequencies
- No access to repeaters

CB Radio

Citizens Band (CB) radios operate on a different frequency band than FRS/GMRS and MURS radios. Without going into specifics, the frequencies used by CB radios are typically less effective at communicating in an urban environment when compared to FRS/GMRS frequencies. Handheld CB radios are significantly larger than FRS/GMRS and MURS radios, making them less than ideal for a bug-out bag.

Pros

- Affordable
- No license required

Cons
- Limited range
- Larger than other handheld two way radios
- No access to repeaters

Ham Radio

The ham radio has played an integral role in every disaster this nation has faced for over 100 years. Ham will remain functional even when modern-communication devices become worthless. The seemingly old-fashioned devices are extremely reliable and allow users to connect with the outside world when Internet, cell towers, and phone land lines are no longer functional.

Worldwide, people regularly communicate with one another through a frequency spectrum on amateur radios. Operators of ham radios number in the millions, which means you can potentially get in contact with people from numerous geographic locations. Probably one of the best things to have for an emergency is a two-way, ham radio. Basically, the way it works is by using the VHF or UHF band and as an added bonus, it will pull in weather band as well. If you don't have a ham-radio license, you can only use it to receive and you will not be able to legally transmit, unless it's an emergency. It's nice to be able to pick up everything with this device: fire, police, local EMS, etc., so that you can hear everything that is going on in your area, as well as communicate with other hams with a license.

Whether this is your first time exploring the world of ham radios or you've been doing this for several years, purchasing a radio depends on what you'll use the radio for as well as your budget. People often overlook handheld and mobile devices due to their limited capabilities compared to larger, stationary setups. Portable ham radios cater more to the amateur and hobbyist and are ideal for emergencies and short-range communication. However, the limited size impacts its battery life, which also shortens the device's range. You can use mobile transceivers in cars or in a fixed station, and they typically come with better ranges and supported frequencies.

In order to use FM repeaters and simplex channels, your portable ham radio must be capable of sending communication on these popular frequencies. In the world of ham radios, accessing these repeaters is necessary to reach other individuals on their own devices. The most popular radios are dual-band, meaning they can transmit on both 2-meter and 70-cm bands. This means you can listen to one band while transmitting on the other, increasing your ability to effectively communicate with multiple operators.

Power is imperative because it impacts the handheld ham radio's communication range. Successfully hitting repeaters and making simple contacts require a device with enough output power to send the signal. Your geographic location is factored into the power levels of a device. Being around flat, open areas naturally requires less power. The typical radio should be capable of 3-5 watts of output power to adequately send a signal.

The Baofeng is an extremely popular, quality, portable, ham radio that has become a prepper staple. It is durable and is amazingly inexpensive. When you look at the price they're asking for, a five-star rating hardly seems to be enough. This is a fantastic value! For fewer than forty bucks, you get a pocket-sized, dual-band radio, complete with earphone/mike and a desktop, drop-in charger.

The Baofeng is rechargeable and can hold a charge for about 12 hours. You can buy a larger, rechargeable battery pack for it on eBay or Amazon, as well as one that accepts AAA batteries. A third option consists of a cigarette-lighter car charger that glides on the back of the radio. I use rechargeable AAA batteries in mine so that I am not reliant on an A/C outlet in order to recharge it. I use the Goal Zero Guide 10 Plus Solar Recharging Kit to keep my batteries charged. This way I can be on-the-go and not held back by the grid.

I feel that the use of a ham radio is an urban-survival must. It does take some time in order to learn how to operate and program, but it is well worth the invested energy. It doesn't come with user instructions (if you can believe that), but there is plenty of information on YouTube, in books, and on various websites solely dedicated to ham radio use.

Recommended Websites

- *www.arrl.org* (The American Radio Relay League (ARRL) is the national association for amateur radio)
- *www.eham.net* (the Internet's #1 Amateur Radio Community)
- *Qrz.com* (Think of it as the phone book for radio amateurs. Most licensed hams around the world have an entry in QRZ)
- *Hamradio.net* (world's largest supplier of amateur/ham radio and communication equipment)
- *Swap.qth.com* (biggest ham radio classified on the web)
- *http://www.radioreference.com/apps/db/* (frequency database for the entire U.S.)

Pros

- Greatest range out of handheld, two-way options
- Access to ham repeaters, which are common in most areas
- Ham radio has scanner capabilities, unlike the other two-way radio options
- Inexpensive for the Baofeng brand
- Ham radio is there when all other forms of communications fail
- Can use AAA batteries with different battery case.

Cons

- Complicated
- Requires a license test and fee
- License only grants use to one person
- Requires multiple family/group members to learn to use in order to be an effective communication strategy

Using Stealth to Operate an Amateur Radio

Because ham radio people are a crafty lot (and some places don't allow antennas), there is a whole sub-genre of ways to make antennas so they can't be detected (by sight, not by signal). Antennas can be made out of flagpoles, ladders, fences, railings, and a lot of other things in plain sight. They can also be hidden inside things or buried.

There are several books such as:

- *Low Profile Amateur Radio: Operating a Ham Station from Almost Anywhere*
- *Stealth Antennas (This is a British book geared to that area of the world, but most of the ideas are universal.)*
- *Stealth Amateur Radio: Operate From Anywhere (*This is one of the best books on the subject.)

With the proper knowledge (which you can really only get with practice), you can make a radio out of stuff that you can find pretty much anywhere. Not only is this useful in the way of hiding your antennas, it could seriously come in handy if you had to make an antenna in a pinch, such as during an emergency.

Obviously, the more experience you have with radios, the easier it'll be for you to do something of this nature.

Once again, there are many different ways to communicate during a disaster situation, but for the most flexible and effective way, you should seriously look into getting your ham-radio license and start playing around with its use. It's a great hobby and one that could mean the difference between finding your family in an emergency or losing them.

19
3-3-3 RADIO PLAN

Survivalist-Communicator 3-3-3 Radio Plan

This is the "when, where, and how" to make radio contact with each other when needed most. The "3-3-3 radio plan" was designed for communications during a crisis. Versions of it are used by survivalists, preppers, and emergency-communications groups. It is based on the easy-to-remember "survival rule of three." It is often called a radio schedule or a SKED.

ABOUT THE 3-3-3 RADIO PLAN

Here's how the 3-3-3 radio plan works: Turn on your radio . . . every 3 hours . . . for 3 minutes . . . on Channel 3.

WHEN: EVERY 3 HOURS

Always use your local time for local area communications with the 3-3-3 radio plan. At the top of the hour, every 3 hours: 12, 3, 6, 9, around the clock, 24 hours a day (AM/PM).

HOW LONG: FOR 3 MINUTES

At the top of every 3rd hour, turn on your radio. Even if you don't need to make a call yourself, always turn on your radio and listen for calls for at least 3 minutes. This is because you never know if someone may be trying to reach you or may need help. If you need to check in, make a short transmission at this time. Say "This is me, just checking in." If you have sufficient battery power, or if you haven't connected in for a while, then you should listen for 15 minutes.

ACCURATE TIME KEEPING

Synchronize your watch with others whenever possible. If you doubt your watch accuracy, compensate by keeping your radio on for a longer duration, before and after every 3rd hour. If you don't have a watch, try listening to an AM-broadcast radio station; they always identify their call letters at the top of each hour.

WHERE: CHANNEL 3

Channel 3 usually applies to CB, Family Radio Service (FRS), or Multi-Use Radio Service (MURS). These are the most common types of radios used by preppers. If your group has a different designated channel or prepper-ham frequency, you should use it instead of Channel 3. The rest of the 3-3-3 radio plan remains the same. Keep it simple.

HOW: FEATURES OF THE 3-3-3 RADIO PLAN

- Easy for everyone to remember
- Conserves precious battery life
- Gets everyone on the air at the same time
- Sets a schedule for 8 times per day for calling in
- Avoids impractical hourly schedules
- Enables the use of short transmissions for optimum success and security
- Three hours of rest in a survival situation
- A person can walk 8 miles in 3 hours, the practical distance limit of handheld radios over average terrain.

The 3-3-3 survival rule is a well-known principle in survivalist-training communities. It commits fundamental skills or procedures to memory. The 3-3-3 radio plan builds upon the survival rule of 3 (otherwise known as the rule of threes).

Unable to keep time

An alternative to the 3-3-3 radio plan, if you have lost track of time of day due to watch or clock failure, is called the "sun-based radio plan" and it uses a three-times daily "sunrise, noon, sunset" schedule, and the "listen interval" is approximately 45 minutes to an hour for each contact. The sun is the timekeeper.

Local "noon" is the observed time when the sun is highest in the sky. The contact time for sunrise starts when the sun is just peeking above the horizon. The contact time for sunset starts while the sun is setting. If you are in a valley or in mountainous terrain, you must compensate and estimate the real sunrise and sunset. During inclement weather, the sun position is estimated, normally by observation of the color of the light. An additional night schedule may be added, and this is normally determined by the position of a star constellation, agreed upon in advance or by a radio message.

The sun-based radio plan is especially useful for high-frequency (HF) communications because it takes advantage of the natural-daily changes in ionospheric reflection. It is also convenient for communication while traveling or camping since the scheduled contacts at sunrise and sunset are normal in-camp times.

Plausible Scenarios

Let's take a look at a list of plausible scenarios that could lead to the need for emergency commun-ication.

- Normal communications fail for unpredictable duration

- Electronic-communications-infrastructure disaster
- Massive computer virus or attacks render damage to the Internet
- Electrical-grid failure causes eventual failure of electronic-communications infrastructure
- Adverse weather, geologic, or natural disaster causes infrastructure failure
- Manmade disaster or unrest brings partial or widespread infrastructure failure
- Regional/local infrastructure blackouts or brownouts
- Restrictions or adverse consequences on the use of the normal communications infrastructure
- Any of the above in combination may lead to a domino effect of unpredictable chaos for communications-infrastructure failure

20
MORSE CODE

In the 1890s, Morse code began to be used extensively for early radio communication, before it was possible to transmit voice. In the late nineteenth and early twentieth century, most high-speed international communication used Morse code on telegraph lines, undersea cables, and radio circuits. In aviation, Morse code in radio systems started to be used on a regular basis in the 1920s.

The main benefit to using and knowing Morse code is the ability to send messages over long distances (hundreds or thousands of miles) on a relatively low amount of power. There are actually some amateur radios that require only a couple AA batteries to communicate with Morse code.

Morse code can be extremely useful in emergencies, and has been used by the military and ham radio operators for years.

When it comes to alternative languages, Morse code is probably the best known, particularly for survival. After all, even people who know nothing about preparedness or Morse code still know the old "SOS" emergency signal. However, few people really know this valuable language well enough to communicate beyond that simple phrase, which means that it is important that you learn it and are ready to use it during any major emergency.

After all, when rescue teams are searching around to assist people or if you need to communication around to assist people or if you need to communicate somewhat confidentially, what better form of communication can be used other than Morse code?

SOS

By far, the most commonly known signal for "help" is the SOS call. You can use other things beside the whistle to send an SOS (such as lights or flags), but the code is still the same: three dots, three dashes, and three more dots. The dot is a short, sharp pulse about three seconds long; a dash is a longer pulse, approximately six seconds long. When calling an SOS signal, keep repeating the signal as often as you can stand it, and for as long as you need it.

The SOS is the internationally recognized distress signal in Morse code, and over the years SOS became associated with such phrases as "save our ship", "save our souls," and "send out succor." Yet, the odd truth is that SOS does not actually stand for anything. In fact, SOS is only one of several ways that the combination could have been written. Using the code VTB would produce exactly the same dots and dashes, but for whatever reason, SOS was chosen to describe this combination. SOS is the only 9-element signal in Morse code, making it easily recognizable, since no other symbol uses more than 8 elements.

This distress signal was first adopted by the German government in radio regulations effective April 1, 1905, and became the worldwide standard under the second International Radiotelegraphic Convention, which was signed on November 3, 1906 and became effective on July 1, 1908. SOS remained the maritime radio distress signal until

1999, when it was replaced by the Global Maritime Distress and Safety System.[1]

International Whistle Codes
Three blasts of the whistle is an international distress call, which is loosely translated as "help me!" Two blasts of the whistle are a call-back signal, meaning "come here." One blast can mean "where are you?", or it can be a call-back signal if you hear anything that sounds like a code. Each whistle blast should last 3 seconds.

Learning Morse Code
Although you can read the chart below to learn the alphabet in Morse code, it won't do you much good without knowing how to properly transmit or how each letter actually sounds.

Visit *http://www.learnmorsecode.com/*. This site has an excellent series of audible guides that will help you hear the letters and numbers, which is generally a more useful, faster, and effective manner of learning Morse code. Also, in North America, many thousands of individuals have increased their code recognition speed (after initial memorization of the characters) by listening to the regularly-scheduled, code-practice transmissions broadcast by W1AW, the American Radio Relay League's headquarters station.

Many educators will advise that the best way to learn a language is to listen first to a phrase, then associate the meaning, and lastly pronounce the phrase or response. Unfortunately, when an individual is along trying to learn Morse code, the try and true is difficult to implement. The frustration comes when the student attempts to key a word or phrase and has no direct feedback as to whether the keying was correct. A novel invention called the Magic Morse Code Trainer Kit eliminates this barrier to learning by providing immediate feedback and in a manner that would be the way a trained listener would recognize the keying. By providing positive and immediate feedback, the student learns to key correctly and can spend more effort on accuracy and rhythm. This kit can be purchased on Amazon for around $40.

A cheaper and probably more likely method of learning and using Morse code in this modern day and age would be to use a smartphone app. Surprisingly, there are several very useful ones available that will provide you with study guides, translators, games, decoders, and Morse code/SOS flashlight transmitters. There are also multiple computer software applications that are similar to these apps as well.

Morse Code Transmission Tips

- **Don't send faster than you can receive**. This helps experienced listeners avoid spamming out letters at newbies who are still trying to learn and is also a helpful way to say "slow down" without needing to know how to type that out. Furthermore, remembering this rule keeps you from going too fast for the message to be written down, which is the usual method of understanding Morse conversations.
- **Have basic practice under your belt before transmitting to the wider world**. Many ham-radio operators use Morse code for fun, and broadcasting imperfect, slow,

and generally unintelligible drivel clogs up the airways. By all means listen, even if you have little skill, but try to have at least a basic grasp before broadcasting yourself.

- **Use the minimum power needed to communicate**. This is actually part of FCC rules for anyone broadcasting, and it has a practical aspect as well, since overpowered broadcasts can interfere with TVs and other devices. If "transmitting" by banging on rocks or flashing lights, variations on this rule could apply in order to minimize the chance of others hearing or seeing what you are doing.

- **Be brief**. Morse code is not often translated at faster than 20 words per minute. This makes a true conversation extremely tedious and annoying. As such, many "Q Codes" (so named because all begin with the uncommon letter Q) have been developed and are in common usage. It is usually expected that users can identify most of these codes, particularly ones related to using Morse code itself, since they offer similar convenience that "text speech" does to phone users. Even with these codes, try to keep conversations very short, in order to prevent those you are communicating with from becoming irritated.

- **Be Patient**. Get used to a slower pace with Morse code. It just comes with the territory. You're probably going to be reduced to communicating by banging a rock on a wall or manually flashing lights anyway, so don't get anxious, otherwise you'll probably mess up sending/receiving the messages.

The Alphabet

I actually hesitate to add a Morse code , visual alphabet here since it could potentially slow learning, but then it can be advantageous to print it out for those who simply don't know Morse code and need to quickly transcribe a simple message. However, probably an easier method still would be to use the Morse code graph tree that is subsequent to this.

International Morse Code

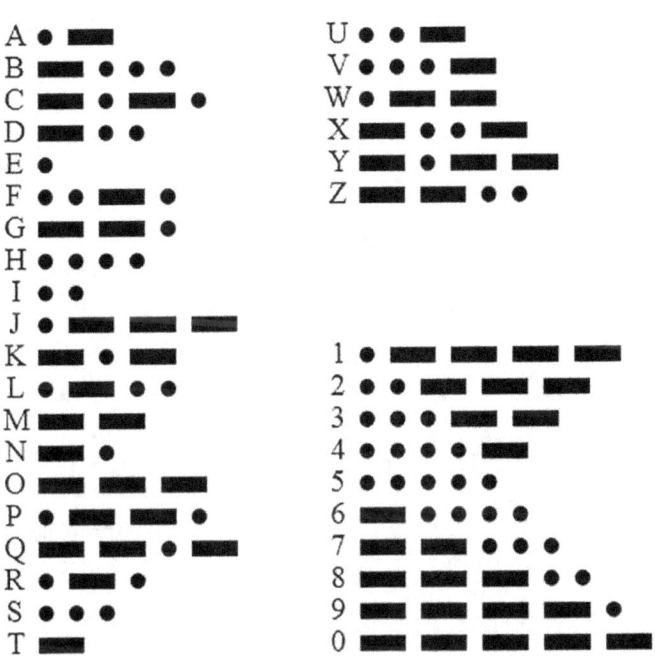

Morse Code Learning Graph

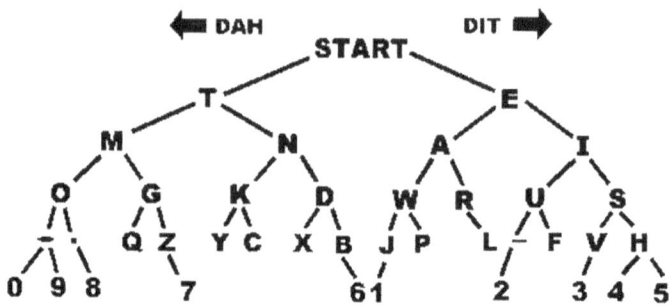

1. Print out this Morse code graph tree on your printer.
2. Place your pencil where it says START and listen to Morse code.
3. Move down and to the right every time you hear a DIT (a dot).
4. Move down and to the left every time you hear a DAH (a dash).
5. An example would be "DAH DIT DIT," which is a dash then dot then dot. To try this example out, again place your pencil at the START position. When you hear a DAH, move down and left to the T, and then when you hear a DIT, move down and RIGHT to the N, and when you hear another DIT, move DOWN and RIGHT again and land on the D.
6. You then write down the letter D on your code copy paper and jump back to START waiting for your next letter.

The key to learning the code is hearing it and comprehending it while you hear it. The only way to get there is to practice 10 minutes a day.

Listen to code tapes or computer practice code while tracing out this chart and you will find yourself writing down the letters in no time at all without the aid of the chart. The chart brings repetition together with recognition.

Secondary use

Although common Morse code is known and used by a significant population of hams, adapting a "secret code" from that language is quite easy and more difficult to riddle out. Abbreviations and certain phrases can all mean different things, giving you a convenient and simple way to dialogue without giving information out to any curious or sinister listeners. Just remember not to use abbreviations or codes with non-group members. (You don't want to confuse others you're communicating with that are not part of your crowd.)